MY DEAD DAD
WAS IN ZZ TOP

MY DEAD DAD WAS IN ZZ TOP

★ ★ ★ ★ ★ ———— ★ ★ ★ ★ ★

100% REAL,* NEVER-BEFORE-SEEN DOCUMENTS FROM THE WORLD OF ROCK AND ROLL

JON GLASER

With a Foreword by Ira Kaplan

*100% Fake

HARPER ⬤ PERENNIAL

NEW YORK • LONDON • TORONTO • SYDNEY • NEW DELHI • AUCKLAND

HARPER ● PERENNIAL

FIRST EDITION

Designed by Patrick Borelli

Library of Congress Cataloging-in-Publication Data is available upon request.

ISBN 978-0-06-174962-9

11 12 13 14 15   RRD   10 9 8 7 6 5 4 3 2 1

For Leslie, Nathan,
and my as-this-was-going-to-print-still-alive father

"I bought a ticket to the world,

But now I've come back again.

Why do I find it hard to write the next line?

Oh, I want the truth to be said."

—SPANDAU BALLET

☆ FOREWORD ☆

R egrets, I've had a few, but then again too few to mention. Words to live by, whether you come to that sentiment via Frank Sinatra (whose birthplace of Hoboken, New Jersey, has been my home for decades) or Sid Vicious or even Paul Anka (if you have never heard the recording of him berating his band, put down this book immediately—after paying for it, of course—and seek it out). But I do have one regret I'd like to share with you.

Time was I proofread books for a cheapo paperback publisher. Most of my assignments were sexy postapocalyptic survivalist dramas and sexy Old West cowboys and Indians dramas, but on one occasion I was given a compendium of rock 'n' roll trivia to correct. This book was riddled with mistakes to a laughable degree, and my regret is that I didn't xerox the thing in its original form, because all these years later the only example of its slapdashitude I can recall is a reference to Maria Muldaur's 1974 hit record "Midnight at the Oasis" as "Meet Me at the Oasis." Which I concede doesn't seem that funny, but I'm a stickler for accuracy.

As such, and keeping in mind the Pythagorean theorem ("Once a proofreader, always a proofreader"), it was with no small amount of foreboding that

I picked up Jon Glaser's *My Dead Dad Was in ZZ Top*. In this age of Wikipedia and Internet rumors repeated until they are mistaken for fact, I suspected yet another contribution to the noise that's making truth so paradoxically difficult to discern amidst the overload of information. A section devoted to names that my group allegedly considered before deciding on Yo La Tengo was not a good sign. I have no memory of any of these names.

And yet . . . and here's where Glaser has separated himself from your print-the-legend rabble. Through an awe-inspiring amount of research, he has found documentation to back up even the most outrageous of the claims within. In the case of Yo La Tengo, he has somehow located a piece of paper in which those rejected names appear, and I cannot claim that it is not my handwriting, because it most unmistakably is. One must thereby conclude that all of the other stories in this book, no matter how dubious, are, as the subtitle promises, "100% Real."

By now, I hope you've enjoyed that Paul Anka tirade and have once again picked up *My Dead Dad Was In ZZ Top*. I invite you to sit down in a comfortable chair and "Meet Me at the Oasis"—the oasis of Knowledge!

—Ira Kaplan

☆ INTRODUCTION ☆

Hello. Welcome to *My Dead Dad Was in ZZ. Top.* It was a long and arduous journey to get here, one that required a lot of blood, sweat, tears, and—as you will find out later in the book—a little bit of cum. And while I would like nothing more than to say that this book was a labor of love and that it was all worth it, I cannot, because it was not. It was anything and everything but. It was a labor of pain. And heartache. And betrayal. And anger. And resentment. And shock. And sadness. And stress. And more pain. And more anger. Walls were punched. A soul was searched (not mine). Animal ears were scritched and scratched to help soothe frayed nerves. It was never easy to get to the truth. I had to bribe. I had to blackmail. I had to bribemail. Let this serve as a warning to anyone reading this—be he man, beast, machine, or the female versions of those (woman, she-beast, womachine)—who is considering embarking on his or her own quest for knowledge: pure truth comes at a heavy, heavy price. For every dollar this journey cost me, it cost me thousands more in emotion dollars.

The inspiration for the entire book is the following set of letters that you are about to read. These letters require a bit of a preamble and explanation, which begin with the passing of my father several years ago.

I will do my best to condense a lifetime's worth of pain into a few short paragraphs.

I didn't know my dad very well. My parents divorced when I was quite young. My father and I had what I will generously call a peripheral and strained relationship. Rarely there for Little League games. Cards on birthdays. That sort of thing. When I found out he was sick and that it was terminal, I thought for sure that we would be able to find some way to resolve any outstanding issues and put our differences behind us. At the very least, I thought we would be able to establish a sense of closure and resolution, so he could die—and so I could move on and live—in peace. Unfortunately, not only did this not happen, but what unfolded after his death only served to allow him to continue to torment me from the grave.

I traveled back to Michigan to settle his estate. Various items to be sold or donated were packed into boxes. Other items, long since stored and in need of inspecting and appraisal, were taken out of boxes. It was a very profound experience, to say the least, getting to know my father through his possessions, trying to piece together the man I never really knew. I saw photos, books, plaques from various jobs, articles of clothing, so many things I had never seen. One of the things I discovered about him that I never knew, a piece of information that he figured wasn't worth sharing with his only son, was that he was in ZZ Top. Not the band as we know it—he's not part of the main trio. He was in an earlier incarnation of the band.

In a box marked "Do Not Show This To My Son," I discovered a stack of letters that he had written to the guys in the band. There were dozens, but I will share the four that I feel best sum up his experience. Or perhaps they're just the four that best sum up the father that I always longed and ached for. In any case, without further explanation, here they are. The inspiration for the whole journey.

The ZZ Top Letters.

HEY GUYS, BY NOW YOU KNOW THAT INSTEAD OF TALKING ABOUT STUFF AT THE REHEARSALS, I PREFER TO KEEP QUIET, GATHER MY THOUGHTS AT HOME, AND WRITE YOU ALL LETTERS. I KNOW YOU HATE IT AND WOULDN'T PUT UP WITH IT IF I WEREN'T THE GREATER HOUSTON AREA'S BEST KEYBOARD PLAYER. ANYWAY, GREAT REHEARSAL LAST WEEK. I KNOW YOU'RE NOT SUPPOSED TO COUNT YOUR CHICKENS BEFORE THEY HATCH, BUT I THINK WE'RE GOING TO BE **HUGE!** I MEAN COME ON, WHAT A LINE-UP. BILLY ON GUITAR, DUSTY ON BASS, FRANK ON DRUMS, AND DAVE GLASER ON KEYBOARD. YOU GOTTA BE KIDDING ME. WE'LL BE HOUSTON'S BIGGEST SOUL-FUSION QUARTET IN NO TIME.

DAVE

HEY GUYS. I'M SORRY TO THROW SOME NEGATIVE VIBES YOUR WAY WITH THINGS GOING SO WELL RIGHT NOW, BUT I HAVE TO SAY THAT I **HATE** THE NAME THAT WE DECIDED FOR OUR BAND. ZZ TOP? I HAVE NO IDEA WHAT THAT'S SUPPOSED TO MEAN, AND I STILL HAVE NO IDEA WHAT THE "Z'S" STAND FOR, EVEN AFTER BILLY EXPLAINED IT FIVE TIMES.

BUT I DO HAVE TO SAY THAT I AT LEAST LIKE THE "TOP" PART OF ZZ TOP. SO I'M SUGGESTING THAT WE DROP THE "Z's" AND FOCUS ON THE "TOP" PART.
HERE ARE SOME BAND NAMES I THOUGHT OF:

TIP TOP
THE TIP TOPPERS
TOP HAT
TOP THIS
TAKE IT TO THE TOP
DESSERT TOPPING
THE FOUR TOPPINGS
SPIN-TOP-SPIN
STRAIGHT TO THE TOP OF THE WORLD
THE ON TOP OF OLD SMOKEY'S
TOP TOP TILL YOU DROP
          AND FINALLY
TT **ZOP** (SORRY GUYS I COULDN'T RESIST PUTTING IT IN)

I HAVE MORE NAMES, BUT WE CAN JUST
GO OVER THOSE AT REHEARSAL.
BUT GIVE IT SOME THOUGHT GUYS.
ZZ TOP IS LAME.

P.S. I SAW THAT MOVIE 'MIDNIGHT
     COWBOY' AFTER REHEARSAL.
DON'T BOTHER SEEING IT UNLESS YOU'RE
INTO WEIRD PORNO'S

                    DAVE

FIRST OF ALL, I CAN'T BELIEVE YOU
DIDN'T LIKE ANY OF MY BAND NAMES.
EVEN SOME OF THE OTHER ONES FROM THE
LIST

TOP O' THE MORNIN
BAD TIPPERS GOOD TOPPERS
WHEN THE RED RED ROBIN GOES TOP TOP TOPPIN ALONG
STOP SIGN MINUS THE 'S'

BUT I'VE BEEN OUTVOTED, AND I'LL GO WITH IT.
JUST DON'T EXPECT ME TO SMILE TOO MUCH
DURING OUR SHOWS.

NOW MOVING ON TO THE SUGGESTIONS OF
US ALL GROWING BEARDS. MANICURED,
STYLIZED BEARDS THAT GO DOWN TO THE
MIDDLE OF THE CHEST. PALEEEEZE!
THERE'S NO WAY WE'LL GET ANY BACKSTAGE
VAGINA WITH THOSE THINGS. I'M GLAD AT
LEAST FRANK AGREES WITH ME ON THIS ONE.
IF YOU GUYS WANT TO GO AHEAD AND GROW
THEM, BY ALL MEANS, BE MY GUEST. JUST
DON'T GO LOOKING FOR ANY APARTMENTS
IN VAGINAVILLE, CAUSE THERE WONT BE
ANY VACANCIES

I'M SORRY TO HOLD SUCH A HARD LINE
ON THIS ONE, BUT I DON'T LOOK GOOD

WITH A BEARD, AND SOMETHING THAT LONG
WOULD JUST GET IN THE WAY OF ME TRYING
TO PLAY MY KEYBOARD ANYWAY. SO THANKS
BUT NO THANKS. I'LL JUST KEEP MY
PONYTAIL. JUST DON'T BE SURPRISED WHEN
I'M THE ONLY BAND MEMBER WHO SMELLS
LIKE VAGINA. IT'LL BE FROM ALL THE
VAGINA I'M GETTING.

DAVE

WELL, I'M SURE THIS WILL COME AS NO SURPRISE, BUT I'M QUITTING THE BAND. THIS ONE WAS A NO-BRAINER, AS THIS IS NO LONGER THE TYPE OF BAND I WANT TO BE IN. I WANT TO BE IN A SOUL-FUSION BAND. I'VE MET WITH SOME MUSICIANS THE LAST COUPLE WEEKS, AND DECIDED TO FORM A BAND WITH A SAX PLAYER NAMED BLUE MO, AND A BASS PLAYER NAMED SKEETS DING DONG.

WE'RE GOING TO CALL OURSELVES SOULFUSCIOUS. IT'S A PLAY ON THE NAME OF THE PHILOSOPHER 'CONFUSCIOUS' WHILE AT THE SAME TIME LETTING PEOPLE KNOW WE'RE A SOUL-FUSION BAND. I THOUGHT OF THE NAME, AND THE OTHER GUYS LOVE IT.

SO THAT'S THAT. I JUST WANT TO SAY THAT I HOPE THERE'S NO HARD FEELINGS. BUT I ALSO WANT TO SAY THAT I'M SO GLAD I'M NOT IN YOUR BAND ANYMORE. I THINK ZZ TOPS IS THE DUMBEST NAME. I THINK THE SONGS SUCK, I HATE ALL OF YOU GUYS AND I HAVE NO DOUBT YOU WILL FAIL WHILE SOULFUSCIOUS ASCENDS TO THE PEAK OF ROCK AND ROLL SUCCESS MOUNTAIN. GOOD LUCK FINDING ANOTHER KEYBOARD PLAYER, A.K.A. THE BACKBONE OF THIS BAND.

DAVE

I found this in one of the boxes of letters.

Me, my sister, and the father we thought we knew.

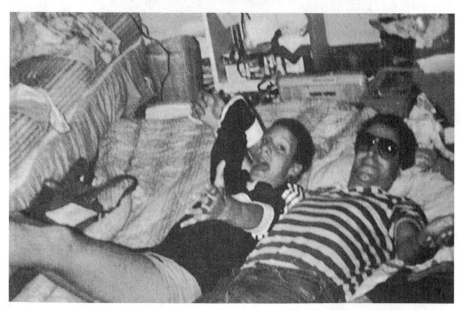

All I can do whenever I look at this photo is wonder how much more fun this moment would have been if I had known my dad was in ZZ Top.

Look how much nerve the liar had to sit with his grandson and pretend he wasn't in ZZ Top and didn't know how to play piano.

So there you have it. These letters—this Pandora's Box (or as I like to call it, Glasedora's Box)—sent a virtual and visceral shockwave of doubt to my very core and disrupted my entire sense of self up to that point in my life. Numb, I began to wonder how many other secrets and lies (not to mention how many copies of Mike Leigh's *Secrets and Lies*) lay boxed up in other estranged fathers' basements. I wondered how many more truths/untruths lay waiting to be discovered within the world of rock and roll. And who better to dig them up than someone whose heart had just been pierced by that very world's dagger of betrayal.

Inspired, I emptied my bowels, filled my belly with a meatball calzone from Lombardi's in Manhattan (the sauce; the bread; the meatballs), and prepared myself to go tear the world of rock and roll a new asshole (giving it a third asshole; rock and roll has two assholes, FYI and BTW). I set out on a fact-finding mission that would span years and continents. The collective results of that mission lay waiting in the remaining pages of this book.

Now it is you who must prepare yourself. To be "me," with the world of rock and roll serving as your father.

MY DEAD DAD WAS IN ZZ TOP

☆ VAN HALEN ☆

When you hear the name "Van Halen," you think of one thing: classic hard rock. The very name "Van Halen" conjures up images of shredding guitar solos, classic front man howling, and a hall of fame rhythm section. Van Halen, Van Halen, Van Halen. It truly is one of the most iconoclastic names in rock and roll. At least, that's what I thought until I traveled to Pasadena, California, and talked to Rick Evans, the band's former lawyer. Get ready to have the doors blown off your dick.

RICK EVANS, esq.
17 Rosebud Lane, St. 8
Pasadena, CA 91101

To: Eddie and Alex Bran Fralen
Fr: Rick Evans
Re: Band name
Date: 4-18-72

Hey, guys. Bad news. I,ve been doing a lot of research
and investigating, and it turns out there already is a band called
Bran Fralen. They're a jazz combo in St. Paul, Minnesota,
consisting of two friends: Hal Bran (sax) and Chris Fralen (drums)
It is my official recommendation that you go with your first
choice from the list of alternates: Van Halen.

I know you guys really wanted to call yourselves Bran
Fralen. It's your last name, and I agree it sounds cool. It
definitely sounds tougher than Van Halen, but what can you do,
that's the way it goes. If it's any consolation, the same
thing happened to Crosby, Stills, and Nash. There were already
three guys named Flosby, Gills, and Lash, who had a fairly
successful acapella group in Dayton. Welcome to the music biz.
This is only the tip of the bullshit iceberg.

Anyway, let me know if that's the name you want to go with.
I think it's the best one from the list of alternates, and it's
already been cleared. Say hi to David and Michael. Oh, and I
listened to the demo for the first album. For what it's worth,
Eddie, Iddon't think you should include "Eruption". Nobody
wants to listen to something that sounds like some asshole
on mushrooms fucking around in their basement.

Ricky

I found this at www.minnesotajazzarchives.com. We had to blur the faces for legal reasons.

☆ KINGS OF LEON ☆

Kings of Leon. Like many bands, they have a fairly interesting sounding name. And like many bands, the story behind the name is a flat out lie. Supposedly named in honor of the band members' father and grandfather, a little digging reveals a far less innocent story, one that involves the rape of the public image of a well-known cultural and sports icon.

RODNEY PORTER, ESQ.

PORTER, DUMARS, AND SALLEY, ATTORNEYS AT LAW
4933 CHANTILLY BLVD. – ST. 4100
LINCOLN, NE 68502

To: Drew Goldman, Atty. at law
Re: Kinks Of Leon Band name
8-14-1999

Mr. Goldman:

My name is Rodney Porter. I represent former heavyweight boxing champion of the world Leon Spinks. It has come to my attention that you represent a band that goes by the name "Kinks Of Leon". I would like to bring your attention to a series of romance novels that carry the same name. In 1981, Leon Spinks began work on what would become the first of a dozen adult-themed romance novels called *"The Kinks Of Leon"*. They followed the romantic, adventure, and sexual exploits of a fictional character named "Leon", loosely based on the champ. I have included one of his more well-known and widely read books, *She Punched My Love*, for reference.

These books have garnered a reputation of being very popular with young, hip crowds for their ironic and "kitch" sensibilities. But make no mistake. This was neither a half-hearted nor an ironic venture for Mr. Spinks. This was something he took very seriously and put a lot of work into, as evident by the number of books he put out, including *Knockout Kisser*, *7ᵗʰ Round Itch*, and *Sexual Sparring Partners*, all under the *Ringside 'Rotica "The Kinks Of Leon"* series brand. It is clear to me that the band "Kinks Of Leon" is trying to capitalize on and exploit the name of Leon Spinks and the literary achievements and recognition he worked so very hard to achieve in *"The Kinks Of Leon"* for their own cultural, personal, and financial gains.

Please consider this a cease and desist order for your band as they now call themselves and instruct them to change their name immediately, or we will take legal action. Thank you.

Rodney Porter

```
                    --THOMPSON TRANSCRIPTION SERVICES--
                               L. SPINKS p1

LEON:    Rodney.  Hey, man, it's Leon.  Hey, man, I saw a sign in a coffee shop last
         week for something that said "Kinks Of Leon".

         (a honking horn is heard)

LEON:    I thought it was for a book signing for me and my books, which seemed fucked
         up since I ain't heard from you about it and haven't done one of those
         things in years.  But I went because

         (honking horn is heard again)

VOICE:   (unintelligible)

LEON:    hold up a sec...

         (yelling to someone)

LEON:    fuck you, man, it ain't green yet!

         (back to the call)

LEON:    Sorry, man, some asshole was honking at me.  Anyway, I went because I needed
         the money (horn honking) and didn't want to let down any fans.  I brought a
         couple copies of

         (horn honking)

LEON:    wait, hold up...

         (yelling at someone)

LEON:    what, motherfucker?!?

VOICE:   (unintelligible)

LEON:    Oh. Oh, hi!

         (back to call)

LEON:    Sorry, man, someone recognized me and was just waving hi.  Anyway, I brought a
         couple copies of Speedbag Or Teabag and She Punched My Love 2 - The Knockout
         Blow, just in case, those are the only books I have left.  Anyway, man,

         (horn honking)

LEON:    I was confused when I got there because there were no books,

         (horn honking)

LEON:    just a bunch of white kids watching a band, and they had "Kinks of Leon"
         written on their drum and

         (horn honking)

LEON:    Wait, hold up

         (yelling to someone)

LEON:    what, motherfucker, I already said hi!  What?  Oh.

         (back to call)

LEON:    I gotta go, now the light turned green for real.  Anyway big Red, please
         give me a call, man, I wanna know what the fuck is going on.
```

*In addition to the lawyer's letter, I also found this transcript of a phone call
between Rodney and Leon.*

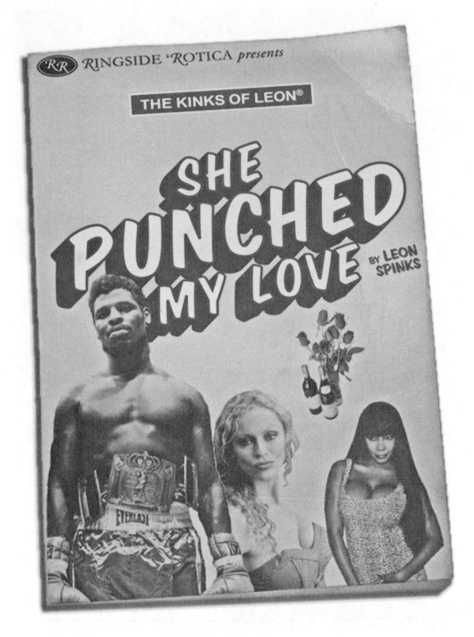

I found an original copy of one of Leon's books. I read it. It was amazing. I won't give away the ending in case anyone ever finds a copy and reads it. But I will say this: (SPOILER ALERT!!!) She actually does punch his love.

☆ THE RUNAWAYS ☆

Formed in the mid-1970s, the Runaways were arguably the first and best all-girl rock band. This was the band that launched the careers of Joan Jett and Lita Ford, after all, and whose bass player ended up in the Bangles. Although there is no denying the group's musical ability, there is also no denying the gimmick factor of an all-girl rock band with a catchy name. However, this was almost a very different band entirely, as this letter to band producer Kim Fowley from his attorney demonstrates.

KEVIN QUADMAN
QUADMAN, DAVIS AND LEOPOLD
49 PICO BLVD., SUITE 402
LOS ANGELES, CA, 90217

Kim:

Hey, buddy. I got your memo. As your attorney, I have to advise
you not to pursue the idea of an all-runaway band called "The Girls".
The legal - not to mention ethical - implications of taking a bunch
of underage female girl runaways off the street and putting a band
together with them, are numerous. You're asking for a lot of trouble.
I know I'm just a nerd who knows the law and not the music biz, but
wouldn't it be a better idea to just take a group of girls who aren't
runaways, and who are musicians, and just call them "The Runaways"?
Do you need actual runaways for this idea? I know it's not as pure of
an idea, but as far as I know, no one in Led Zeppelin is a blimp. No
one in The Doors is a door. No one in Cream is actual cream.

Anyway, in summation, I am advising you to not form an all-
runaway group called "The Girls", and instead, think about forming
an all-girl group called "The Runaways". Or, call them whatever you
want, just don't form a band with a group of underage runaways. Bad
idea, buddy. Bad idea.

KEVIN

☆ THE B-52s ☆

Part punk, part "go-go," part New Wave, part rock, part surf. All original. The B-52s are a band that from the get-go screamed innova-
tion and creativity. Countless kids were undoubtedly inspired by this
band to follow the beat of their own drum. The last thing one could call their
sound would be "pandering" or "commercial." Which made the discovery of
this document all the more surprising, not to mention disappointing.

TO: Fred Schneider

FR: Will Clayton, Sr. Marketing Director, Red Lobster Restaurants,
     Southeast Region

RE: B-52's Red Lobster Proposal

October 11, 1978

Mr. Schneider,

Thank you for your interest in "Red Lobster", and the marketing campaign based on
your band's song "Rock Lobster". I did enjoy the opening verse,

> *Whether lunch or dinner.*
> *Our prices can't be beat!*
> *For the most affordable seafood,*
> *Head to Red Lob-ster!*

However, I don't think that is the angle we here at Red Lobster would like to pursue.
While we do pride ourselves on our affordable, family friendly menu, we like to keep the
focus on the quality of our product. With all due respect, we're not Long John Silvers.

And with all due respect to your band, it's also a little obvious, don't you think?
"Rock Lobster", Red Lobster? It's not the first time we've heard this pitch, but
hopefully it will be the last. I'm sure it won't be if my daughter Tara has any say,
she loves your band. Personally, I don't really get it. You've got an album with songs
about lava, the moon, lobster, and girls. 52 girls, to be specific, which makes no
sense, especially since I only counted 25 girls in the song, which I only know because
Tara has been playing the record over and over and over again for the last month. I
mean, I love our Seaside Shrimp Trio, but there's other dishes on the menu, I don't eat
it every time I order.

Anyway, I digress. Thank you again for your interest in Red Lobster restaurants.
Good luck with a second album, if you get to make one.

Sincerely,

Will Clayton
Sr. Marketing Director, Red Lobster Restaurants, Southeast Region

☆ FLEETWOOD MAC ☆

The "Rumours" are true. Turns out that Fleetwood Mac, a band that seemed way above obvious commercialism, had the almighty dollar in mind as its bottom line.

FROM THE DESK OF
SUSAN STRAWTHORNE
REGIONAL DIRECTOR OF MARKETING

To: Mick Fleetwood
Fr: Susan Strawthorne
Re: Fleetwood Mac Big Mac
March 23, 1978

Mr. Fleetwood.

Thank you so much for getting in touvh with us here at McDonald's.
While I personally am such a fan of the band, I'm sorry to say
that the Fleetwood Mac Big Mac is something that we cannot pursue
at this time.

Yes, we do offer the occasional and/or themed item, such as the
Shamrock Shake for St. Patrick's Day. And your suggestion of
"several slices of Lindsey Bucking-ham, white cheddar cheese
that represents the cocaine Stevie Nicks is addicted to, Mick
Fleet-wood smoked bacon, and John and Christine McVie-al (veal)"
does sound yummy.

But two all beef patties, special sauce, lettuce, cheese, pickles,
onions, on a sesame seed bun seems to work very well for us,
so we're going to stick with that.

Good luck with the band. I LOVED Rumours!!!!!!!!!!!

Sincerely,

Susan Strawthorne

SECRET
SELLOUTS

O ver the days and months and years it took me to put this book together, I noticed several different themes and patterns emerge, some of which you've already seen, and some of which are still to come: journal entries; letters from lawyers; lyric ideas; public inquiries from bands who were willing to sell out their image and sound in exchange for cash. Here now are some not-so-public ideas from bands and musicians who either seemed to be interested in entertaining the notion of selling out, or actually did for smaller businesses that they figured no one would hear about. I'm guessing these bands and musicians would have preferred these never see the light of day. I'm also guessing that I don't give a shit what they think. Enjoy.

☆ BOB DYLAN ☆

Bob Dylan is hands down considered one of the greatest singer/song-writers of his generation, if not all time. His lyrics range from the poetic to the political, and his artistic integrity is second to none. Which is what makes this next set of documents all the more shocking. I found some old lyric journals, and it would appear that Dylan either did some work or thought about doing some work for various advertising campaigns, for both smaller local businesses and bigger national chains. These documents provide some answers that I wish I *hadn't* found blowin' in the wind. Sad.

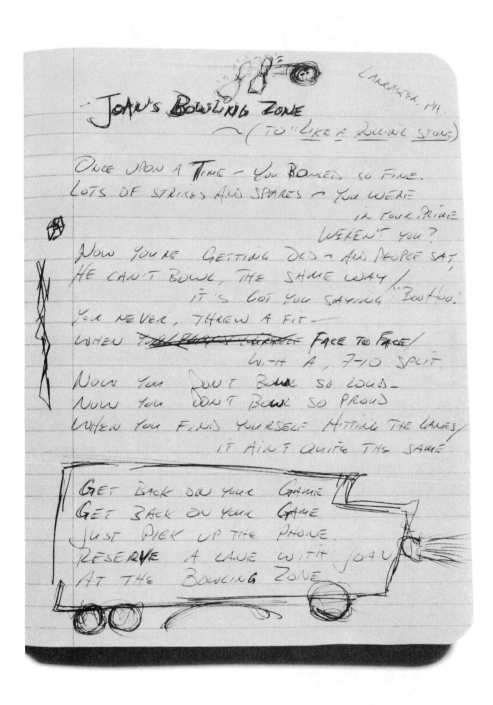

JOAN'S BOWLING ZONE

LANCASTER, PA.

(TO "LIKE A ROLLING STONE")

ONCE UPON A TIME — YOU BOWLED SO FINE.
LOTS OF STRIKES AND SPARES — YOU WERE
                                   IN YOUR PRIME
                                      WEREN'T YOU?
NOW YOU'RE GETTING OLD — AND PEOPLE SAY,
HE CAN'T BOWL, THE SAME WAY /
            IT'S GOT YOU SAYING "BOO HOO."
YOU NEVER, THREW A FIT —
WHEN ~~TOLD YOURSELF~~ FACE TO FACE /
                WITH A, 7-10 SPLIT
NOW YOU DON'T BOWL SO LOUD —
NOW YOU DON'T BOWL SO PROUD
WHEN YOU FIND YOURSELF HITTING THE LANES /
            IT AIN'T QUITE THE SAME

GET BACK ON YOUR GAME
GET BACK ON YOUR GAME
JUST PICK UP THE PHONE.
RESERVE A LANE WITH JOAN
AT THE BOWLING ZONE

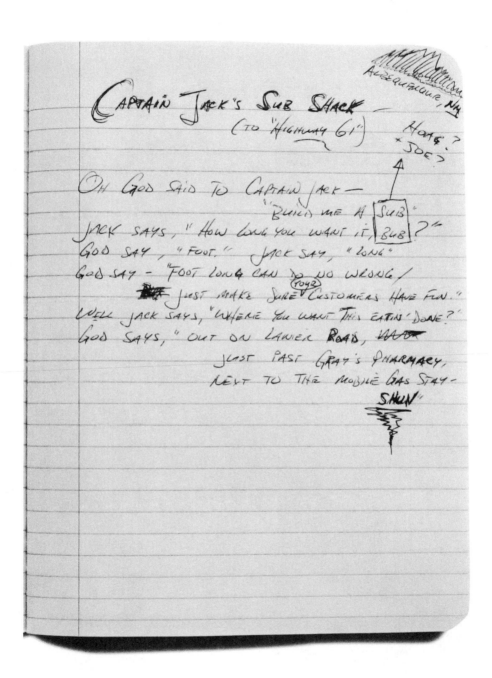

CAPTAIN JACK'S SUB SHACK —
(TO "HIGHWAY 61")

ALBEQUERQUE, NM

HOME?
× JOE?

OH GOD SAID TO CAPTAIN JACK —
"BUILD ME A [SUB]
JACK SAYS, "HOW LONG YOU WANT IT, BUB?"
GOD SAY, "FOOT." JACK SAY, "LONG"
GOD SAY — "FOOT LONG CAN DO (YOUR) NO WRONG/
~~JUST~~ JUST MAKE SURE CUSTOMERS HAVE FUN."
WELL JACK SAYS, "WHERE YOU WANT THIS EATIN' DONE?"
GOD SAYS, "OUT ON LANIER ROAD, ~~~~
JUST PAST GRAY'S PHARMACY,
NEXT TO THE MOBILE GAS STAY—
SHUN"

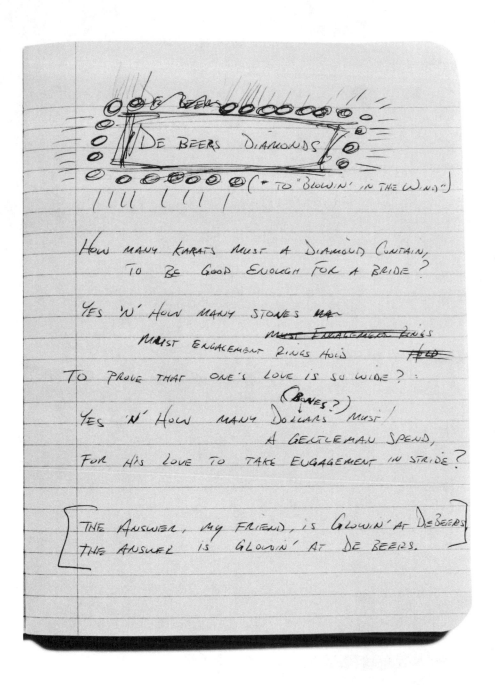

DE BEERS DIAMONDS

(→ TO "BLOWIN' IN THE WIND")

HOW MANY KARATS MUST A DIAMOND CONTAIN,
    TO BE GOOD ENOUGH FOR A BRIDE?

YES 'N' HOW MANY STONES ~~MAY~~
        ~~MUST ENGAGEMENT RINGS~~
    MUST ENGAGEMENT RINGS HOLD   ~~HOLD~~
TO PROVE THAT ONE'S LOVE IS SO WIDE?

            (BONES?)
YES 'N' HOW MANY DOLLARS MUST
            A GENTLEMAN SPEND,
FOR HIS LOVE TO TAKE ENGAGEMENT IN STRIDE?

THE ANSWER, MY FRIEND, IS GLOWIN' AT DE BEERS,
THE ANSWER IS GLOWIN' AT DE BEERS.

☆ DAVID BOWIE ☆

Like Dylan, David Bowie is one of the great musicians of our time, someone whose creative and artistic integrity is matched by very few. And like Dylan, it was a shame to find these journal entries. These are but two of many I found.

CHANG'S GRILL (to "Changes")

Still don't know what I was hungry for,
Hard to choose, what w/a million
    FAST FOOD JOINTS and...
Every time I thought my mind was
    made, my ~~tastebu~~ BUDS OF
    TASTE could not agree
So I forced myself to ~~settle~~, +
I landed on Chinese
When I'm in the mood for ~~Chinese~~
    SOME ASIAN,
THERE's just one place you can
    take me (please)

CHORUS: CH-CH-CH-CH-CHANG'S GRILL!
    (try the fried lo-mein)
    CH-CH-CH-CH-CHANG'S GRILL!
    (the Hunan (human?) ribs are to die for)
    CH-CH-CH-CH-CHANG'S GRILL
    (dim sum + soup + more!)
    CH-CH-CHANG'S GRILL
        their Gen ~~Gucks~~ TSO's
            chicken is best in town...
Just say CHANG ME!
    They're open until nine.
                    DBX

FOR "MATTRESS CITY" (BRIGHTON)
(to "SUFFRAGETTE CITY")

HEY MAN, oh now hear what I said!
HEY MAN — I NEED A NEW BED!
HEY MAN — I need something that's
                          FIRM
I want something good but don't
    have £ (MONEY?) to burn!

_____

HEY MAN! — my old bed's insane!
HEY MAN! — it's causing BACK PAIN;
HEY MAN! — See how the middle doe's
                          SAG!
    You know I tried to ro-tate, but it...
            and then it...
If you need a new bed, w/ a price
        that's ITTY-BITTY
THEN CHECK OUT MATTRESS CITY!
            (SING as "MATT-CHU-RESS")
If you need a NEW BED, whether
    water-KING, FULL, QUEEN,
    OR TWIN-NY,
then check out MATT-CHU-RESS
    CITY
    (It's out of sight...)
    (you'll sleep tight...) DBA

☆ CREAM ☆

What do you do when you're a British supergroup and one of the greatest guitar players of all time is in your band? You sell your music for use at a small-town linen store, that's what.

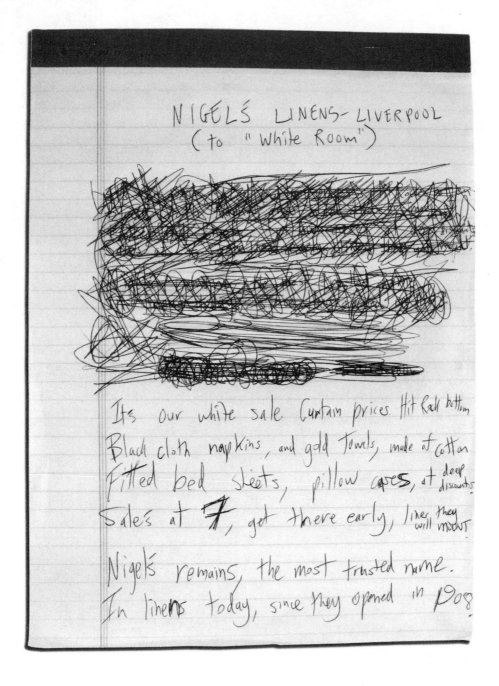

NIGEL'S LINENS - LIVERPOOL
(to "White Room")

It's our white sale. Curtain prices Hit Rock bottom
Black cloth napkins, and gold towels, made of cotton
Fitted bed sheets, pillow cases, at deep discounts
Sales at 7, get there early, liner they will mount

Nigel's remains, the most trusted name.
In linens today, since they opened in 1908

☆ DEEP PURPLE ☆

O kay, so this band doesn't exactly reach the same artistic heights as
the likes of Dylan and Bowie. But they still came up with one of
the most recognizable riffs in rock history. A riff that came very
close to becoming a jingle.

England Boating PSA campaign
(to "smoke on the water")

We know you love your football.
We know you love your fish & chips.
But don't forget we're surrounded by water.
And that means a lot of ships.
So next time you're ~~thinking~~ thinkin'
About a new activity
Maybe think about boating
~~It's lots of fun for you and me~~
Boat on the water, England give it a try.

chorus:

Boating **is** so easy.
Boating is lots of fun.
You can boat with a motor
or you can boat without one.
They come in different ~~sizes~~ sizes.
From large yachts down to the smallest tug.
So whatcha say, England.
~~It's time to catch the boating bug~~
Boat on the water, England give it a try.

chorus

Don't forget to be careful
when you're riding in your boat.
No matter where you do it
On the Thames or in a tiny moat

But that's just a tangent,
and really not the point, you see.
The point is just go get on a boat
And Travel around the deep blue ~~sea~~ sea
chorus Boat on the water, England give it a try.

☆ JETHRO TULL ☆

You'd think that a band whose front man is a flute prodigy prone to seven-minute solos would probably have zero interest in doing anything commercial. And that's just fine, because you'd think that any commercial or advertising ventures would probably have zero interest in that type of band.

VICK'S VAPORUB — (to AQUALUNG?)

SITTING HOME IN BED NOW

got yourself a bad cold, & how

(CHANGE THIS) copyright?

SNOT RUNNING down your nose

ONLY ONE THING to TAKE (I suppose)

sneezing
coughing
Achoo
septum
burning
allergy
sick
fever

VICKS VAPORUB.

Rub all over your chest.

soothes
cures your cold so you can Rest.

VICKS VAPORUB   V V V Vicks VALUE

Soon you're feeling better.

Head outside, just wear A that sweater.

VICKS VAPORUB!

(MAYBE IN COMMERCIAL, guy can play Vicks inhaler like a flute ???)

yes no !!!

UNCLE JERRY'S SOFAS

NOTE: LOCATED IN BRIXTON ENGLAND

(of BUNGLE iN The JUNGLE)

You've GOT a SOFA, but it's getting quite old.
~~You would~~ You'd → like a NEW oNE, or so I have been told.

I KNOW A place where they've GOT A selection,
Of NEW and used SOFAS, GOT quite A collection,
All different ~~prices~~ fabrics, prices, ~~dents~~ at Rock bottom.

You Ask how I KNOW, it's because I just bought oNE.
~~Don't~~ DOWN AT UNCLE JERRY'S SOFAS It's The oNE place to be.

If you Need A, New Sofa.

STop oN IN AND, you'll see,

☆ KISS ☆

Sure, they went commercial later in their careers. But is it possible that one of the most successful, biggest-selling bands worldwide needed to make commercials? It would appear that at some point, they thought they might. Here are a couple PSAs the band wrote.

JUICE PSA
(="TO PEUCE")
WHEN YOU
GET BACK FROM PLAYING OUTSIDE
~~THEN~~ AND YOUR
~~MOUTH~~ THROAT IS FEELING PARCHED
                    AND DRY

THATS WHEN
YOU WANT SOMETHING COLD TO DRINK
~~COCOA~~ WATER IT WILL JUST NOT
                    DO.

AND MILK IT WILL NOT HIT THE
                    SPOT.

YOU KNOW THERES JUST ONE
            THING YOU WANT.

SO GET SOME JUICE.

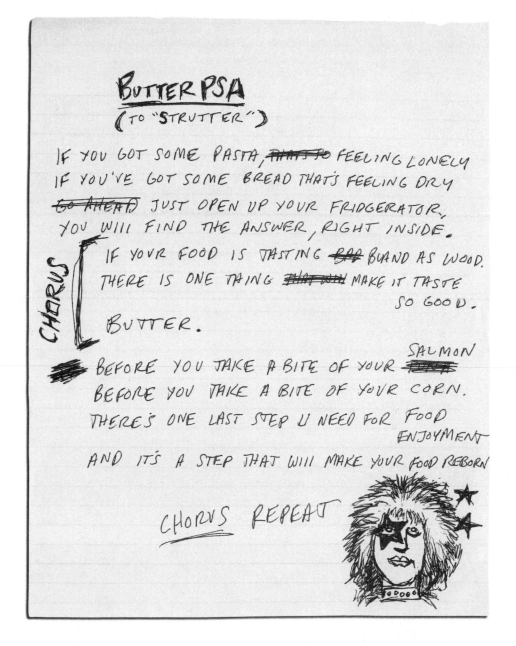

BUTTER PSA
(TO "STRUTTER")

IF YOU GOT SOME PASTA, ~~THATS TO~~ FEELING LONELY
IF YOU'VE GOT SOME BREAD THAT'S FEELING DRY
~~GO AHEAD~~ JUST OPEN UP YOUR FRIDGERATOR,
YOU WILL FIND THE ANSWER, RIGHT INSIDE.

CHORUS
IF YOUR FOOD IS TASTING ~~BAD~~ BLAND AS WOOD.
THERE IS ONE THING ~~THAT WILL~~ MAKE IT TASTE
                                            SO GOOD.
BUTTER.

BEFORE YOU TAKE A BITE OF YOUR ~~FISH~~ SALMON
BEFORE YOU TAKE A BITE OF YOUR CORN.
THERE'S ONE LAST STEP U NEED FOR FOOD
                                    ENJOYMENT
AND IT'S A STEP THAT WILL MAKE YOUR ~~FOOD~~ REBORN

CHORUS REPEAT

Thus concludes the Secret Sellouts section of the book. On to more totally real documents and artifacts I found when I actually traveled the globe and did research and found these things for real over the course of several years.

☆ LED ZEPPELIN ☆

This cocktail napkin appears to show the final two choices for the name of the band. I'm not sure if "Stairway to Heaven" would be perceived as the classic song it is today had the band gone with the other name.

FINAL TWO NAMES

-Led Zeppelin

-Cottonball Goldenstein's Good Time Sunshine Lollipop
Smiley Face
(fart noise)

☆ BRUCE SPRINGSTEEN ☆

Bruce Springsteen is perhaps the quintessential American rock and roll icon. His blue-collar image and songs about Americana have solidified his status as a tough, workingman's musician. Or have they? This cocktail napkin shows a different thought pattern to Springsteen's early lyric mindset, and suggests that perhaps the seminal Springsteen anthem "Born to Run" only ended up as it is because of a few serendipitous spills. People may start thinking of him as Bruce Spills-teen after this.

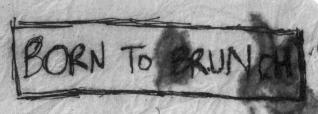

BORN TO BRUNCH

THE DINER'S JAMMED WITH HUNGRY EATERS
ON A LAST MINUTE ~~DRIVE OF~~ LUNCH
EVERY~~BODY'S~~ BODY [JUST WANTS] ~~POWER~~ POWER TO EAT RIGHT NOW
BUT THERE'S NO SEATS LEFT FOR BRUNCH

TOGETHER ~~DIANA~~ NANCY WE'LL LIVE WITH THE ~~HUNGER~~ HUNGER
I'LL LOVE YOU WITH ALL THE BACON IN MY
OMELLETTE
↑ (CHECK SPELLING)

SCAMPS LIKE US,
BABY WE WERE
BORN TO BRUNCH

☆ THE ROLLING STONES ☆

The Rolling Stones are arguably the greatest band in the history of rock and roll. Mick Jagger and Keith Richards are inarguably two of rock and roll's most recognizable and indelible icons. The following documents are about to destroy the veneer surrounding the world's most enduring rock and roll band and, specifically, Mick and Keith.

Mick:

I've been thinking about your idea, that we switch names as a big joke, and I think it's bloody genius, we should absolutely do it. I'll call myself Mick Jagger, and you'll call yourself Keith Richards. I like the name Mick Jagger better for me anyway, it sounds like more of a lead singer name. It will be absolutely hilarious! Who knows how long we'll actually stay together as a band anyway, I'm sure it'll be for just a few months or something, and I'll end up back at the London School of Economics, back to being good ol' Keith Richards, getting my teaching degree. Anyway, hilarious idea, me friend. Can't wait until our first show in a couple weeks. See you at rehearsal!

Yours,

K. R.

Keith (or should I say, Mick!)

Keith,

How bloody hilarious was the gig last night! I almost soiled me trousers when you introduced the band and said "and KEITH RICHARDS on lead guitar"! This is going to be too fucking funny, I'm glad you and the other guys are into it, and I'm glad our friends and family are game. Like you said, we'll probably be a band for just a little while, and then we can go back to our real names. But until then, it'll be ~~hilarious~~ hilarious to pretend that my name is your name and that your name is my name. When we're a couple of old geezers, we'll look

back on this and have a
laugh or two. Or three!
Anyway, mate, this is going
to be fun, see you at rehearsal,

Yours,

Keith

ps. - Don't worry
    Don't worry, mate, I know my
    name is Mick. I'm just signing
    my letter "Keith" to practice
    getting in the habit of being
    used to it.

CUT TO:
48
YEARS
LATER

<u>Will and Testament</u>

<u>Of</u>
<u>MICK JAGGER</u>

I, MICK JAGGER, being of sound and disposing mind, memory and understanding, and after consideration of all persons, the objects of my bounty, and with full knowledge of the nature and extent of my assets, do hereby make, publish and declare this my Last Will and Testament as follows:

1.   <u>FIRST</u>:

I direct all payments, monies and royalties to be split evenly among my children.

2.   <u>SECOND</u>:

I do hereby devise and bequeath each and every thing of value of which I may die possessed, including real property, personal property, and mixed properties, to be split evenly between Anita Pallenberg and Patti Hansen, as detailed with the law firm of Gedrich, Masoni and Furlstein.

3.   <u>THIRD</u>:

Let it be known that my real name is Mick Jagger, not Keith Richards. Keith Richards, who you may know as Mick Jagger, and I decided to play a joke and switch names when we were very young and just starting off with our band, the Rolling Stones. Very quickly, things spiraled beyond our control, and there was no going back. Only those closest to us knew, and those people by now have taken our secret to their graves. People were deceived, and people will

WILL OF MICK JAGGER

- 1 -   _____
                                          MJ

undoubtedly be shocked and hurt to discover this news, but it is true. I
just want to make sure I officially put it to paper in case I am to die before
getting the chance to tell the truth. So there you have it. Mick Jagger is
really Keith Richards, and Keith Richards is Mick Jagger. Try wrapping your
head around that one, world.

I subscribe my name to this Will this <u>20</u> day of August, 2009, at Turks & Caicos.

Mick
_____
                          MICK JAGGER

WILL OF MICK JAGGER
            - 2 -   _____
                                                  MJ

☆ ELTON JOHN ☆

Elton John is one of music's great all-time performers. With a career spanning four decades, John has sold more than 250 million records and had seven consecutive number-one U.S. albums, fifty-seven Top 40 singles (twenty-seven in the Top 10), four number-two hits, and nine number-one hits. He has won five Grammy awards, an Academy Award, a Golden Globe Award, a Tony Award, and was inducted into the Rock and Roll Hall of Fame in 1994.

Much of his success, it must be said, has to be attributed to his songwriting partner, Bernie Taupin. Theirs is widely considered to be a legendary pairing in the pantheon of music and songwriting. Also of note is the pair's remarkable songwriting process. Taupin writes the lyrics on his own. When he is finished, he hands them off to John, who then sets the lyrics to music. They do each task separately, never working together, and never working in the same room the entire time. They have done this for every song they worked on. Except one.

Here now is the never before seen lyric sheet that both Taupin and John worked on together, in the same room. Guessing from the lyrics that Taupin usually writes, it seems like a fairly safe bet which lyrics and handwriting/pen ink are John's.

Together (IN THE SAME ROOM!)
By Elton John and Bernie Taupin
April 17, 1973

Hey. Here we are.

Sittin' together. IN THE SAME ROOM.
I gather strength from your presence
JUST LIKE A CAR GO ~~VROOM~~. ZOOM →

Hey. Here we are.
Sittin next to

Sittin' here side by side.
LIKE TWO SEA SHELLS AT LOW TIDE.
(OR: JUST LIKE GROOM AND BRIDE?
- BONNIE AND CLYDE?
- PRETENDING WE'RE GOING FOR A RIDE.
- TAKING IT ALL IN STRIDE.
- LIKE A PLANE THAT STARTS TO GLIDE.
- IT WAS THREE OF US BUT ONE DIED.
BERNIE - LET'S COME BACK TO THIS ONE
LATER AND FIGURE IT OUT)

So many things that I wanted to say,
But I could never find the words.

You know who else can't find the words?
BIRDS. 'CAUSE THEY CAN'T SPEAK (HUMAN) WORDS.
JUST BIRD WORDS.

WHAT DID YOU HAVE FOR BREAKFAST?

I HAD TWO EGGS AND TOAST.
BACON AND JUICE, AND CRAP OL EGGS ALSO
ALSO SOME GRITS.
AND THEN I GOT REALLY FULL.

(BERNIE — I DECIDED AGAINST RHYMING
WITH 'TOAST', SOMETIMES ITS FUN TO
<u>NOT</u> RHYME STUFF)
THOUGHTS??

And even in the rarest of moments,
When we should find ourselves apart,
The thought of you, will always find v
through,
As I hold you dear to my heart FART

I KNOW THIS IS
CHILDISH, BUT MAYBE
WE CAN TRY IT?

LOLA
LAYLA
L????A

I n June of 1970, the Kinks released what would go on to be one of the all-time great rock and roll songs: "Lola." Six months later, Derek and the Dominoes would release another song that would go on to be considered one of the greatest songs in rock and roll: "Layla." Throughout the following year, 1971, a handful of other bands, sensing a trend, shamelessly tried their hand at songs about girls with similar-sounding names. For obvious reasons, these songs were never released. And for other obvious reasons, it's a shame they weren't.

☆ MC5 ☆

Leela

Went out to the bar, I met a cute girl
She told me, "I want to feel ya!"
I looked in her the eye, I asked, "What's your name?"
And she told me that her name was Leela.

Leela!! oh Leela!!
Can our love be for real, huh?
Leela!! oh Leela!!
I will never forget her name.

Tuesday with
Ben Francisco -
Carpenter

Hard to believe this was written by the same people who proclaimed "Kick out the jams, motherfucker!" But I like the ring of "Kick out the jams, Leela!"

☆ GRATEFUL DEAD ☆

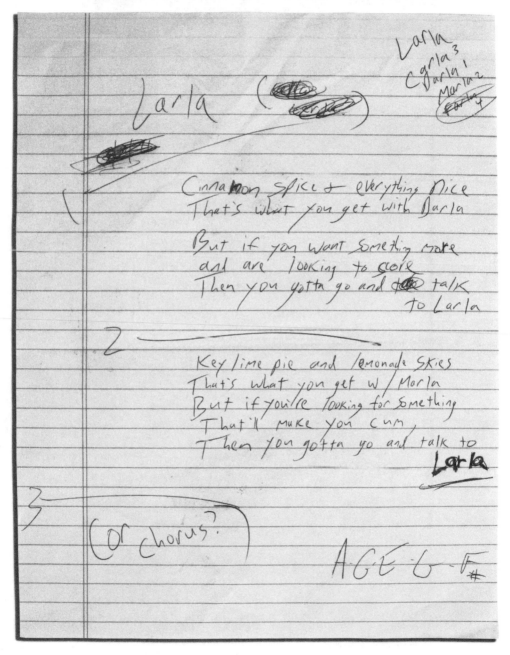

Larla
Larla₃
Carla₁
Marla₂

Larla

Cinnamon spice + everything nice
That's what you get with Larla

But if you want something more
and are looking to score
Then you gotta go and talk
                    to Larla

2

Key lime pie and lemonade skies
That's what you get w/ Marla
But if you're looking for something
That'll make you cum,
Then you gotta go and talk to
                              Larla

3

(or chorus?)

A·C·E·G·E#

This has a real "Sugar Magnolia" vibe to it. Except for the part about cum.

☆ ALICE COOPER ☆

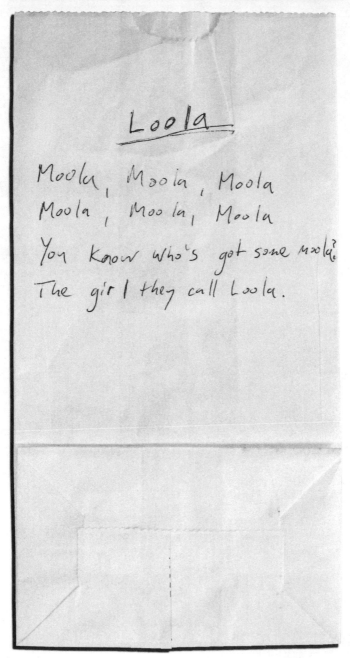

It's almost as if he were writing this from the perspective of the protagonist from "I'm Eighteen."

☆ T. REX ☆

"LULU"

LULU, MY SWEET LULU

L ALWAYS BE TRUE TO YOU KNOW WHO

LULU, MY SWEET LULU

YOU'RE MY SPACEY ASIAN LADY VERSION
OF STAR TREK'S SULU

I could actually see this one being a hit with just the right amount of T. Rex treatment applied to it. Shame Marc Bolan didn't try; Lulu could have been his "20th Century Girl."

☆ SANTANA ☆

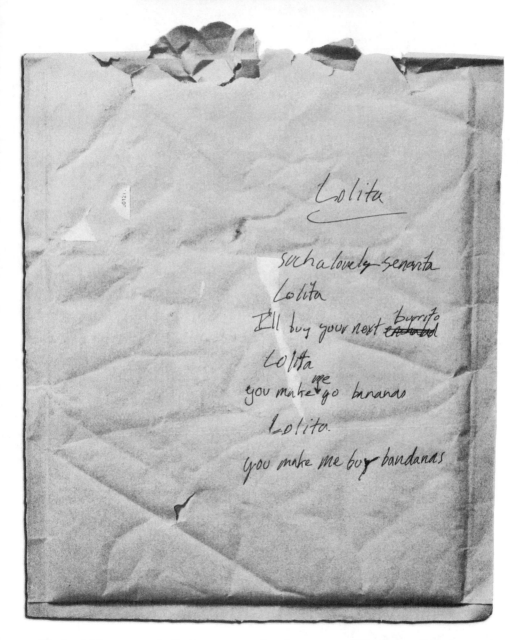

Lolita

such a lovely senorita
Lolita
I'll buy your next ~~enchiled~~ burrito

Lolita
you make me go bananas

Lolita.

you make me buy bandanas

He should have recorded it. I want to go buy bananas and bandanas right now.

On November 14, 2004, Steven Spielberg's daughter Rachel was bat mitzvahed. The musical act? None other than Prince himself. A highly respected artist known for his unwillingness to compromise his vision, Prince altered the lyrics of some of his songs to give them a more Jewish feel. To ensure that no one knew about the performance, Mr. Spielberg and Prince signed an agreement of full nondisclosure. Guests apparently also had to sign a waiver of secrecy to never talk about that night. Here now is the never-before-seen set list from that night.

THANK YOU'S: STEVE, KATE

MAH-ZEL TAHV   TO RACHEL

I COULD NEVER TAKE
THE PLACE OF YOUR RABBI

RASPBERRY YARMULKA

WHEN DOVES KVETCH

LITTLE RED DRAIDLE

I WOULD DIE 4 YOUR GEFILTE FISH

THIEVES IN THE SYNAGOGUE

SEXY POTATO LATKE

PURPLE OY VEY

THE BEAUTIFUL CHOSEN ONES

I WANNA BE YOUR CANTOR

GETT OFF (THE BEMA)

☆ THE BEATLES ☆

After the Beatles broke up in 1970, one member of the band had a harder time letting go than the others.

Apple
3 Savile Row, London

Fr: Ringo
To: The rest of the Beatles
Re: Post-band project
April 17, 1970

Hey lads,

It's me, your old mate Ringo! Can you believe it was only a week
ago that we were all still Beatles? I was walking down the street
just the other day, and some tourist came up to me and said"Hey.
Aren't you a Beatle?" And I said "Yes." A few seconds later I
realized that in fact I wasn't a Beatle anymore, but when I turned
around to tell the poor bloke, he was already gone. Oh well. Guess
I need to get used to telling people I'm not a Beatle after being
a Beatle for so long.

Anyway, that's not what I'm writing to tell you. I have some news,
and I wanted textall you all to hear it first from your old mate
Ringo.

I know it's only been a week since Paul officially announced the
break up of the band, but I wanted you to be the first to know
that I am immediately starting up a Beatles tribute band. I have
a feeling people are still hungry for the Beatles, and I think
this is a good way to give them the music without us actually
being a band anymore and playing shows for them. And they'll
bexx still be able to see one actual Beatle! (well, former
Beatle, anyway).

I don't know how you will feel about this, but I can only hope
you will all give your blessings to an old mate. Here is a list
of names I'm thinking about. If anyone has a problem with any
of them, please let me know:

    Peppered Sergeant
    The Paperback Rockers
    Twisty and the Shouters
    Jude and the Heys
    I, Me, Mike and the Taxmen
    Yellow Six Foot Party Sub
    Dizzy Lizzy Monkey's Hideout
    Doc Robert and the Come Together Blackbirds
    Prudence and the Good Day Sunshine Gang
    Eavesdrop Eddie and Wantin' To Know A Secret
    Cry Baby Goldman and the Weepy Guitars
    Ding Dong Ringo and the Hand Holders

Apple
3 Savile Row, London

And here are a few specialty versions I was thinking of:

Oy Vey Truffle (klezmer versions)
Chopped Liverpool (another klezmer idea)
And Your Bird Has Dreadlocks (reggae versions)
Fool on the Ska (ska versions)
I Yam What I Yam the Walrus (we all dress as Popeye)

Anyway, mates, let me know what you think. Oh, and if anyone needs anyApple Records stationary, let me know. As you can see, I managed to steal a few pads on me way out the door!

Yer old mate,

Ringo

P.S.   I miss being a Beatle!

☆ THE WHITE STRIPES ☆

The true nature of the relationship between Jack and Meg White is a much debated rock and roll urban legend. Are they brother and sister? Are they former husband and wife? Here now is a telegram which, once and for all, shines the light of truth on a truly amazing story.

PATRONS ARE REQUESTED TO FAVOR THE COMPANY BY CRITICISM AND SUGGESTION CONCERNING ITS SERVICE

WESTERN UNION

CLASS OF SERVICE

This is a full-rate Telegram or Cablegram unless its deferred character is indicated by a suitable sign above or preceding the address.

NEWCOMB CARLTON, PRESIDENT   J. C. WILLEVER, FIRST VICE-PRESIDENT

SIGNS

DL = Day Letter
NM = Night Message
NL = Night Letter
LCO = Deferred Cable
NLT = Cable Night Letter
WLT = Week-End Letter

The filing time as shown in the date line on full-rate telegrams and day letters, and the time of receipt at destination as shown on all messages, is STANDARD TIME.

Received at

Dear Mom/Meg:

You may want to sit down. I'll give you a minute to find a place
to sit. Okay, you're probably sitting by now. When you are ready,
continue to the next telegram.

THE QUICKEST, SUREST AND SAFEST WAY TO SEND MONEY IS BY TELEGRAPH OR CABLE.

PATRONS ARE REQUESTED TO FAVOR THE COMPANY BY CRITICISM AND SUGGESTION CONCERNING ITS SERVICE

CLASS OF SERVICE

This is a full-rate Telegram or Cablegram unless its deferred character is indicated by a suitable sign above or preceding the address.

WESTERN UNION

NEWCOMB CARLTON, PRESIDENT   J. C. WILLEVER, FIRST VICE PRESIDENT

SIGNS

DL = Day Letter
NM = Night Message
NL = Night Letter
LCO = Deferred Cable
NLT = Cable Night Letter
WLT = Week-End Letter

The filing time as shown in the date line on full-rate telegrams and day letters, and the time of receipt at destination as shown on all messages, is STANDARD TIME.

Received at

Okay, here goes. The young man who just knocked on your door and hand delivered the very note you are reading right now, was in fact none other than your son Jack. Jack White. Me. I know you are going to find this hard to believe, which is why I wrote this and delivered it in the first place. I figured it would be easier for you to digest it this way, although I'm sure you still won't believe this to be true.

THE QUICKEST, SUREST AND SAFEST WAY TO SEND MONEY IS BY TELEGRAPH OR CABLE.

WESTERN UNION

CLASS OF SERVICE

This is a full-rate Telegram or Cablegram unless its deferred character is indicated by a suitable sign above or preceding the address.

NEWCOMB CARLTON, PRESIDENT   J. C. WILLEVER, FIRST VICE PRESIDENT

SIONS

DL = Day Letter
NM = Night Message
NL = Night Letter
LCO = Deferred Cable
NLT = Cable Night Letter
WLT = Week-End Letter

The filing time as shown in the date line on full-rate telegrams and day letters, and the time of receipt at destination as shown on all messages, is STANDARD TIME.

Received at

I'm 25 years old, and I'm from the future. To make a long story
short, I asked a scientist friend of mine to help me out and he
built a sports car called a DeLorean into a time machine and then I
drove this car back here to the year 1974, in September, the month
before I was conceived. I have come here on a mission. I want to
start a two-piece rock and roll band, and I need a drummer. I've
been holding auditions for quite some time now, and no one is working out. I've been racking my brains for the last few months
trying to think of someone that might be a good fit, and it finally
hit me.

WESTERN UNION

NEWCOMB CARLTON, PRESIDENT   J. C. WILLEVER, FIRST VICE-PRESIDENT

CLASS OF SERVICE	SIONS
This is a full-rate Telegram or Cablegram unless its deferred character is indicated by a suitable sign above or preceding the address.	DL = Day Letter NM = Night Message NL = Night Letter LCO = Deferred Cable NLT = Cable Night Letter WLT = Week-End Letter

The filing time as shown in the date line on full-rate telegrams and day letters, and the time of receipt at destination as shown on all messages, is STANDARD TIME.

Received at

I started thinking about how you always talked about wanting to be
a drummer but didn't have the time once I was born. I remember the
story you told me about flipping a penny. "Heads" you'd pursue
playing the drums for a living, "tails" you'd have a baby. It's
hard to think of a coin flip as a one-cent abortion, but I have
spent a lot of time thinking about how if that coin had landed on
'heads', I wouldn't be here today. I figuratively wouldn't be here
today, alive, and I literally wouldn't be here today, asking my mom
to come back to the future and play drums in my band.

WESTERN UNION

Received at

I know you didn't mean it to be, but that story has been quite a burden of guilt to carry around all these years. My albatross. But don't feel bad, Mom/Meg. I bear no grudge or ill will. If anything, it has fueled and inspired me to figure out the best way to give back to the one person who sacrificed so much for me. So I have come to ask you to come back with me to the future and be a drummer. My drummer. In our band.

Together (IN THE SAME ROOM!)

By Elton John and Bernie Taupin

April 17, 1973

Hey. Here we are.
Sittin' together. IN THE SAME ROOM!
I gather strength from your presence.
JUST LIKE A CAR GO ~~VROOM~~. ZOOM

Hey. Here we are.
~~Sittin' next to~~

Sittin' here side by side.
LIKE TWO SEASHELLS AT LOW TIDE.
(OR: JUST LIKE GROOM AND BRIDE?
   —BONNIE AND CLYDE?
—PRETENDING WE'RE GOING FOR A RIDE.
—TAKING IT ALL IN STRIDE.
—LIKE A PLANE THAT STARTS TO GLIDE.
—IT WAS THREE ~~OF~~ US BUT ONE DIED.
BERNIE— LET'S COME BACK TO THIS ONE
   LATER AND FIGURE IT OUT)

So many things that I wanted to say,
But I could never find the words.
YOU KNOW WHO ELSE CAN'T FIND THE WORDS?
BIRDS. 'CAUSE THEY CAN'T SPEAK (~~HUMAN~~) WORDS.
   JUST BIRD WORDS.

I would have gone with "Like Hakeem Olajuwon and Clyde the Glide."

Totally real fact: On January 1, 1966, Marco Hietala, bass player for the Finnish rock group Nightwish, was born.

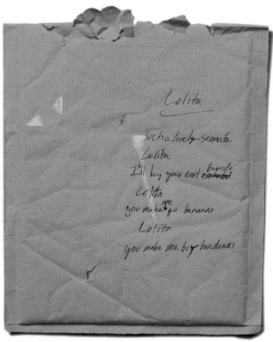

Lolita
such a lovely señorita
Lolita
I'll buy your next ~~enchilada~~ burrito
Lolita
you make me go bananas
Lolita
you make me buy bandanas

Maybe this envelope was a delivery of black and magic bandanas. Maybe Santana was trying to think of a song, opened the envelope, and started writing. Hey, who knows. AM I RIGHT????

Since it closed, the space has been a furniture store, a massage parlor, a strip club, and four different Arby's franchises.

Love the ink color. Who knew Jesus's favorite color was Vatican blue? I thought it would have been something more humble, like brown or olive, or some other earth tone. Whatevs, Jesus.

Jonfucius say: "Red letter look nice against faded gray, but turquoise would have been twice as nice." Whogivesafuckfucius do not care what Jonfucious think.

SECRETARIAT OF STATE

FROM THE VATICAN, 7 June 1988

Hi, Jim and William.

I have contacted The Vatican and asked The Holy
Father to transcribe and forward this to you.
I am writing to object to the name of your band.

(Before I go any further, let me just say that I
am a huge fan. Love, love, LOVE your guys' sound.
Psychocandy will undoubtedly go down as one of the
most influential, seminal post-punk albums of all
time. Darklands was a brilliant follow up effort,
„Fall" was a standout song for me)

In any case, I just have to be honest and say that
I'm not crazy about the name you've chosen. Don't
get me wrong. I get it. It's ironic, it's edgy,
I'd even say it's clever. But I'd appreciate it if
you'd please reconsider for any albums from here
on. I can't make you change the name, but I'd really
appreciate it. I have instructed His Holiness to
pray for you and future successes for your band.

Okay, okay, take it easy, Jesus, you've said your
piece! 'Preciate your time, and good luck. I'm
excited to hear what else the brothers Reid have in
store for the music loving public!

Anxiously awaiting more but also STRONGLY urging you
to change your name,

Jesus

P.S. - Lose the drum machine. Borrrrr-ing!

God, I loved that shirt. It caught fire on a sparkler on July 4, 1976. Thankfully, I was not wearing that sweet vest at the time.

My favorite yellow Patagonia shorts. They put the "short" in shorts, and the "hugger" in "dick huggers."

So curious to know what lyrics about fine linens didn't make the cut.

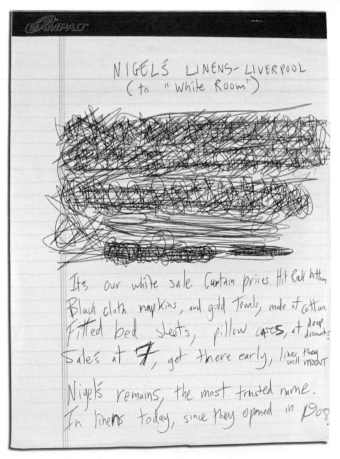

NIGEL'S LINENS - LIVERPOOL
(to "White Room")

Its our white sale Curtain prices Hit Rock bottom
Black cloth napkins, and gold Towels, made of cotton
Fitted bed sheets, pillow capes, at deep discounts
Sales at 7, get there early, lines they will mount

Nigel's remains, the most trusted name.
In linens today, since they opened in 1908

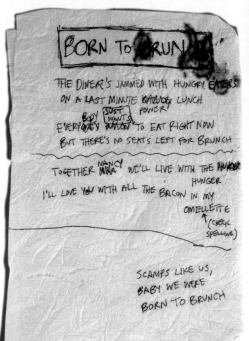

I appreciate the Blue Note-esque cover design. I also appreciate the shitty album title these two blurred, smug dickhead fuckface assholes came up with.

Guessing by the color, the spill looks like some kind of Thai hot sauce. Or maybe the Boss likes mixing his ketchup and mustard. I'm surprised he didn't write a song called "Ketchtard Cadillac."

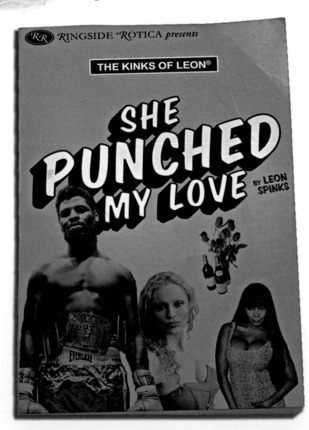

What's not to like about this cover? It's here so you can see the nice orange/blue color scheme.

This is the hat I took took the patch from. If this patch was, say, fake, and I had, say, ordered a bunch of them online, I could probably sell them on a website or blog or something. I bet a lot of people would love to have that patch. Too bad it's totally real and one-of-a-kind.

It's always amazing to see super-old documents that have been around for more than two hundred years.

To Mr. Paul Weller:

Good day to you sir. I hope this letter finds you well, as I trust it will.

Let me just begin by saying that what you are about to read will undoubtedly be difficult to comprehend. All I can do is give you my word that every word of it is the truth.

My name is Thomas Jefferson. As you may or may not know, I was the third President of the United States of America. I was was also the principal author of the Declaration of Independence, and indeed, it was I who penned the passage. "We hold these truths to be self-evident, that all men are created equal; that they are endowed by their Creator with certain unalienable Rights, that among these are Life, Liberty and the pursuit of Happiness."

Red Lobster®

TO: Fred Schneider

PR: Will Clayton, Sr. Marketing Director, Red Lobster Restaurants,
    Southeast Region

RE: B-52's Red Lobster Proposal

October 11, 1978

Mr. Schneider,

Thank you for your interest in "Red Lobster", and the marketing campaign based on
your band's song "Rock Lobster". I did enjoy the opening verse,

> Whether lunch or dinner.
> Our prices can't be beat!
> For the most affordable seafood,
> Head to Red Lob-ster!

However, I don't think that is the angle we here at Red Lobster would like to pursue.
While we do pride ourselves on our affordable, family friendly menu, we like to keep the
focus on the quality of our product. With all due respect, we're not Long John Silvers.

And with all due respect to your band, it's also a little obvious, don't you think?
"Rock Lobster", Red Lobster? It's not the first time we've heard this pitch, but
hopefully it will be the last. I'm sure it won't be if my daughter Tara has any say,
she loves your band. Personally, I don't really get it. You've got an album with songs
about lava, the moon, lobster, and girls. 52 girls, to be specific, which makes no
sense, especially since I only counted 25 girls in the song, which I only know because
Tara has been playing the record over and over and over again for the last month. I
mean, I love our Seaside Shrimp Trio, but there's other dishes on the menu, I don't eat
it every time I order.

Anyway, I digress. Thank you again for your interest in Red Lobster restaurants.
Good luck with a second album, if you get to make one.

Sincerely,

Will Clayton
Sr. Marketing Director, Red Lobster Restaurants, Southeast Region

Judging by the coffee or chewing-tobacco stain, Mr. Clayton obviously didn't give a shit when he sent the letter. Or maybe it was Fred Schneider's coffee or chewing tobacco.

I would have thought Warhol might go with a different color, or colors: maybe red for the meat, green for the lettuce, more of a brown for the bun, etc. Happy and sad at the same time that it's yellow.

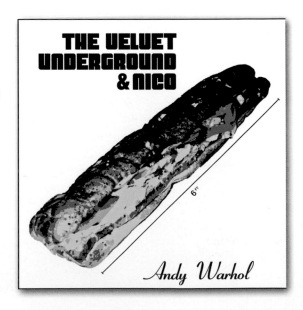

I just read that Eric Stoltz was originally the drummer in the White Stripes.

WESTERN UNION

Received at

I'm 25 years old, and I'm from the future. To make a long story
short, I asked a scientist friend of mine to help me out and he
built a sports car called a DeLorean into a time machine and then I
drove this car back here to the year 1974, in September, the month
before I was conceived. I have come here on a mission. I want to
start a two-piece rock and roll band, and I need a drummer. I've
been holding auditions for quite some time now, and no one is working out. I've been racking my brains for the last few months
trying to think of someone that might be a good fit, and it finally
hit me.

STAPLES   Signa

England Boating PSA Campaign
(to "smoke on the water")

We know you love your football.
We know you love your fish & chips.
But don't forget we're surrounded by water.
And that means a lot of ships.
So next time you're ~~thinkin~~ thinkin'
About a new activity
Maybe think about boating
~~It's lots of fun for you and me~~
Boat on the water, England give it a try.

chorus!

Boating is so easy.
Boating is lots of fun.
You can boat with a motor
or you can boat without one.
They come in different ~~little~~ sizes.
From large yachts down to the smallest tug.
So ~~whatcha~~ say, England.
~~It's time to catch the boating bug~~
chorus Boat on the water, England give it a try.

Don't forget to be careful
when you're riding in your boat.
No matter where you do it.
On the Thames or in a tiny moat

It says on Wikipedia that Staples was founded in 1986, but that is obviously not true.

My Dearest Christian,

As junior year comes to a close, my heart is filled with both love and sadness. It is filled with love because I have the affections of a wonderful young man. Its filled with sadness because unfortunately, that young man is no longer you. Gary Darkness asked me to prom last week, and I have decided to go with him. I know that you and I have been sort of going out for a few weeks, but Gary's a senior, and...... Oh Christian, I'm ~~SO~~ sorry. I'd be lucky to go to prom with either of you, but I really think Gary could be "the one" Argh, this is so hard!!! I guess the only way to say this is just to say it: Christian, I love you, but I've Chosen Darkness. I'm going to prom with Gary. I'm ~~SO~~ sorry. I really hope we can still be friends.

Stacy

xoxoxox

THANK YOU'S: STEVE, KATE
MAH-ZEL TAHV TO RACHEL

I COULD NEVER TAKE
THE PLACE OF YOUR RABBI

RASPBERRY YARMULKA

WHEN DOVES KVETCH

LITTLE RED DRAIDLE

I WOULD DIE 4 YOUR GEFILTE FISH

THIEVES IN THE SYNAGOGUE

SEXY POTATO LATKE

PURPLE OY VEY

THE BEAUTIFUL CHOSEN ONES

I WANNA BE YOUR CANTOR

GETT OFF (THE BEMA)

Just wanted people to see that Prince writes in purple ink.

I love how girly some girls are when they're being all girly. Even when they're breaking your fucking heart to go out with Gary.

AT LAST.

"Let them eat cake"
—Marie Antoinette, France

CAKE LOVERS! CRUISES
THE FIRST CRUISE LINE FOR PEOPLE WHO LOVE THE SEA, AND CAKE.

ANGEL FOOD • ATLANTIC OCEAN • BIRTHDAY • ... GERMAN CHOCOLATE • CARIBBEAN SEA • BUNDT • PUGET SOUND

UPCOMING 1990 CRUISES!

BAHAMAS
3 DAYS
FEATURING
Butter Pound Cake
Chocolate Chiffon
Jelly Roll
Vanilla Sponge Cake

ALASKA
4 DAYS
FEATURING
Devils Food Cake
Lemon Poppyseed
Raspberry Bundt
Angel Food

...peace and tranquility you desire from a trip at sea, ...ed with all the sugary sweetness and bliss you crave ...n delicious cake. All in one cruise. Cake Lovers Cruises. ...rst cruise line for people who love the sea. And cake.

You want luxury? Look no further than our impeccably designed Aquaria Suites. Open your window to a world of water and wonder. Feel the ocean's breeze softly cascading along your face as the finest, moistest cakes pass through your lips. Suites come in a variety of sizes, ranging from our 250 square foot Sea Horse suites, to our massive 1500 square foot Neptune suites. No matter the size, all rooms are fitted with the finest beds and linens. You'll appreciate the attention to every detail, from bamboo floors, to the cake shaped faucet handles. And no mint on the pillow here. Every night, you'll return to an immaculately clean room with a personalized cup cake waiting for you on your goose down pillow.

"Let them eat cake.
On a cruise ship!"
—Carolyn M., Hilton Head, South Carolina

Leave your worries and troubles behind as they evaporate into thin air and dissolve into the passing sea breeze as you luxuriate on deck. Whether grabbing some rays, or wiping some (cake) glaze (from your mouth), total relaxation is just one bite away. Swim a few laps in our Olympic size pool. Putt for par on one of our half dozen putting greens. Check out a movie. Take in a show. And no matter what you do or when you do it, there will always be cakes wherever you go. You will literally be surrounded by cakes.

Come visit our Cakequarium. You'll see the world's finest cakes as you've never seen them before. Under water! We've gathered some of the world's finest pastry chefs and asked them to design some of the most delicious cakes. We then take those cakes and flash seal them in a see-through, air tight, water tight polyurethane prophylactic. They are then placed in our beautiful, state-of-the-art aquarium, located in our 5 Star restaurant, The Sea Gourmand. Whether you're waiting for your table, or simply having a cocktail, you can enjoy the finest cakes floating along side some of the world's most exotic sea creatures.

So come take a bite out of adventure, relaxtion, and the good life.

~ Cake Lovers Cruises ~

This is here so you can enjoy the burst of colors. It's better than eye candy—it's eye cake.

WESTERN UNION

Received at

I understand if this is a lot to take in and think about. Please take all the time you need to figure out what you want to do. I have a time machine, so time is not of the essence. I already have a plan for explaining to the public who you are. We will create a myth, that you are either my sister, or my ex-wife. I know it'll be weird to think about us in those terms, Mom/Meg, but we can't let anyone know that I have a time machine. There are these terrorists trying to obtain some information, and if they find out about it, they will surely go after my scientist friend and try to kill him. So that's the way it'll have to be.

WESTERN UNION

Received at

I love you and I'm glad you had me, but now is your chance to
un-have me and live the life you always wanted. So whaddaya say?

Much love,

Your Son/Jack

☆ THE SEA AND CAKE ☆

The Sea and Cake has always claimed that its odd, random-sounding name came from drummer John McEntire's misinterpretation of the Gastr del Sol song "The C in Cake." This old brochure from a now defunct cruise line explains the real reason.

ANGEL FOOD • ATLANTIC OCEAN • BIRTHDAY • MEDITERANNEAN SEA • GINGERBREAD • PACIFIC OCEAN • CHOCOLATE • BERING STRAIT • DEVIL'S FOOD • INDIAN OCEAN • ALMOND CHIFFON • GULF OF MEXICO • PUGET SOUND • BUNDT • CARRIBEAN SEA • GERMAN CHOCOLATE • TIERRA DEL FUEGO • CARROT • RED VELVET • PANAMA CANAL • UPSIDE-DOWN • THUNDER BAY • MOUSSE • GULF OF SAINT LAWRENCE

CAKE LOVERS!

CRUISES

THE FIRST CRUISE LINE FOR PEOPLE WHO LOVE THE SEA, AND CAKE.

CAKE LOVERS! CRUISES

UPCOMING 1990 CRUISES!

BAHAMAS
3 DAYS
FEATURING
Butter Pound Cake
Chocolate Chiffon
Jelly Roll
Vanilla Sponge Cake

ALASKA
4 DAYS
FEATURING
Devils Food Cake
Lemon Poppyseed
Raspberry Bundt
Angel Food

AT LAST.

All the peace and tranquility you desire from a trip at sea, coupled with all the sugary sweetness and bliss you crave from a delicious cake. All in one cruise. Cake Lovers Cruises. The first cruise line for people who love the sea. And cake.

You want luxury? Look no further than our impeccably designed Aquaria Suites. Open your window to a world of water and wonder. Feel the ocean's breeze softly cascading along your face as the finest, moistest cakes pass through your lips. Suites come in a variety of sizes, ranging from our 250 square foot Sea Horse suites, to our massive 1500 square foot Neptune suites. No matter the size, all rooms are fitted with the finest beds and linens. You'll appreciate the attention to every detail, from bamboo floors, to the cake shaped faucet handles. And no mint on the pillow here. Every night, you'll return to an immaculately clean room with a personalized cup cake waiting for you on your goose down pillow.

"Let them eat cake"
—Marie Antoinette, France

"Let them eat cake.
On a cruise ship!"
—Carolyn M., Hilton Head, South Carolina

Leave your worries and troubles behind as they evaporate into thin air and dissolve into the passing sea breeze as you luxuriate on deck. Whether grabbing some rays, or wiping some (cake) glaze (from your mouth), total relaxation is just one bite away. Swim a few laps in our Olympic size pool. Putt for par on one of our half dozen putting greens. Check out a movie. Take in a show. And no matter what you do or when you do it, there will always be cakes wherever you go. You will literally be surrounded by cakes.

Come visit our Cakequarium. You'll see the world's finest cakes as you've never seen them before. Under water! We've gathered some of the world's finest pastry chefs and asked them to design some of the most delicious cakes. We then take those cakes and flash seal them in a see-through, air tight, water tight polyurethane prophylactic. They are then placed in our beautiful, state-of-the-art aquarium, located in our 5 Star restaurant, The Sea Gourmand. Whether you're waiting for your table, or simply having a cocktail, you can enjoy the finest cakes floating along side some of the world's most exotic sea creatures.

So come take a bite out of adventure, relaxtion, and the good life.

~ *Cake Lovers Cruises* ~

☆ THE BUTTHOLE SURFERS ☆

There are many theories as to how the band got its crazy name. Truth: the Butthole Surfers got their name from a secret government program that used a shrinking ray to shrink down Navy SEALs, who would then literally surf inside the buttholes of foreign dignitaries the U.S. government wanted assassinated by way of stealth poisonous injections into the sides of their anus. Here is a formerly classified government document that outlines a mission. As you will see, John Haynes, the father of the Butthole Surfers' lead singer Gibby Haynes, was a Navy SEAL who was killed in the line of duty while surfing the butthole of Idi Amin. The band's name is an homage both to Gibby's father and to the secret military special forces program that ranks right up there with the more widely known special forces like the Rangers, Airborne, and SEALs: the Butthole Surfers Covert Assassination Squad, better known as the Butthole Surfers.

TOP SECRET   SPECIAL HANDLING

THE JOINT CHIEFS OF STAFF
WASHINGTON D.C.

November 12, 1976

MEMORANDUM FOR THE SECRETARY OF THE NAVY

    Subject: Operation Deep Extreme

    1. This special operation has been fully approved by the Joint Chiefs of Staff, and is to be executed immediately.

    2. As outlined, this is to be a covert, "unofficial" operation. Agree with recommendation that operation is to be carried out by Navy SEALs, led by Capt. John Haynes.

    3. SEALs will transport to US base in Greece (classified), where they will all undergo the shrinking process via the cathode titanium demolecular transmogrification laser (CTSL 420X) under the supervision of Naval doctors, as well as ██████████████ Surfboards will also be shrunken down at this time.

    4. Shrunken SEAL team and surfboards will be placed into syringe and transported with normal size SEAL team for extraction into Uganda via airdrop.

    5. SEAL team to rendezvous with Special Agent in Uganda. Agent will escort SEAL team to Kampala.

    6. Amin is scheduled to be given his yearly physical on December 1. SEAL team is to detain attending physician, replace with Special Agent. During prostate exam, Special Agent is to insert shrunken SEAL team into Amin's rectum (heretofore referred to as the "butthole").

    7. Shrunken SEAL team is to surf the butthole of Idi Amin and administer subcutaneous injections of the poison Chloritox 7B.

    8. Upon completion of objective, shrunken SEAL team is to rendezvous with normal size SEAL team at airlift point (CLASSIFIED), where they are to be quadruple sterilized.

    9. Mission Abort will be discretion of team leader, whether it be prior to mission, or during mission (surfing of the butthole).

                For the Joint Chiefs of Staff:

                 GEORGE S. BROWN
                    Chairman
             Joint Chiefs of Staff

1 Enclosure
Memo for Chief of Operations, B-Hole Project

TOP SECRET   SPECIAL HANDLING

TOP SECRET SPECIAL HANDLING

December 10, 1976

MEMORANDUM FOR THE SECRETARY OF THE NAVY

Subject: Final report on failed Idi Amin assassination attempt.

1. Mission was successful up until extraction into Idi Amin's rectum.

2. Several SEALs became entangled in anal hairs, a common occurrence during these missions. Capt. John Haynes became entangled on a hair in such a way that the hair wrapped around his throat and snapped his neck.

3. In an attempt to save Capt. Haynes' life, second in command Lt. Cprl. Ron Davis aborted the mission before shrunken SEAL team could administer Chloritox 7B.

4. They were able to remove Capt. Haynes' body, but were not able to recover his surfboard, which remains in Amin's rectum.

5. Dr. Stuart Bonderman believes there to be zero chance of the surfboard ever re-moleculizing itself to normal size, thus compromising the program and future operations.

6. It is therefore the recommendation of the Joint Chiefs that Idi Amin live the rest of his life with a microscopic surfboard ensnared on the anal hairs of his rectum.

For the Joint Chiefs of Staff:

GEORGE S. BROWN
Chairman
Joint Chiefs of Staff

1 Enclosure
Memo for Chief of Operations, B-Hole Project

I took this patch off an old army hat I found at a thrift store.

BEFORE
THEY
MADE IT

Before famous bands became famous and made millions of dollars, they still had to pay the bills. Here are a few bands that put some of their nonmusic skills to good use.

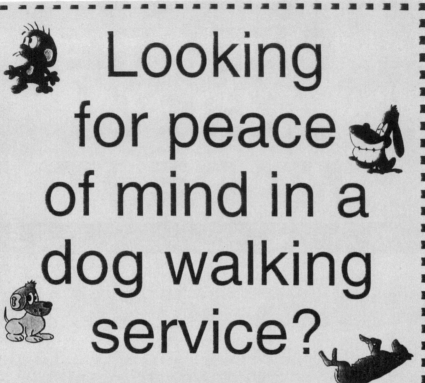

☆ CREEDENCE ☆
☆ CLEARWATER REVIVAL ☆

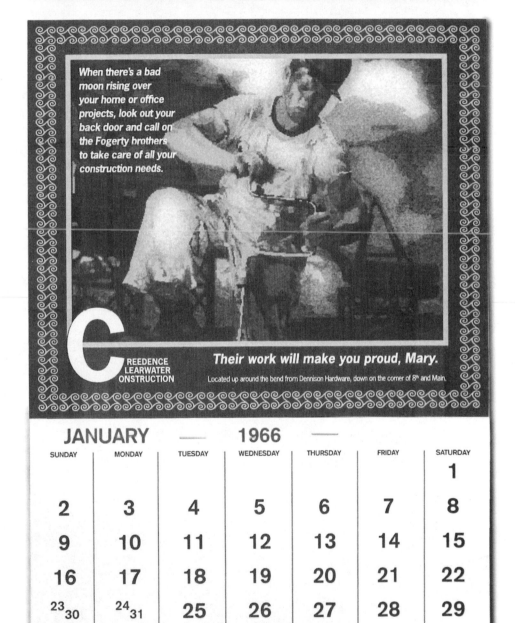

When there's a bad moon rising over your home or office projects, look out your back door and call on the Fogerty brothers to take care of all your construction needs.

CREEDENCE
LEARWATER
ONSTRUCTION

Their work will make you proud, Mary.

Located up around the bend from Dennison Hardware, down on the corner of 8th and Main.

JANUARY — 1966 —

SUNDAY	MONDAY	TUESDAY	WEDNESDAY	THURSDAY	FRIDAY	SATURDAY
						1
2	3	4	5	6	7	8
9	10	11	12	13	14	15
16	17	18	19	20	21	22
23 30	24 31	25	26	27	28	29

☆ **FOREIGNER** ☆

FOREIGNER
Shoe Repair

Bad shoes leaving you hot blooded? Walking on broken heels leaving you with double vision?

Well then say good-bye to all those annoying head games and walk on in to Foreigner Shoe Repair. We'll have your shoes feeling like the first time you wore them. If you want to know what love is when it comes to quality shoe repair, then come on down to Foreigner. Same day service if it's urgent.

HOURS: M-F 10–6 Sat/Sun 12–6
138 Lighthouse Road, Lancaster, PA 17601

☆ MOTÖRHEAD ☆

Your kid a damage case when it comes to math?
Is he finding other tutor's lessons to be overkill?
Then why not give Motorhead Math Tutors *a try?*

While other tutors baby your kids and treat them with no class, we tutor your kids with an iron fist.

We teach them the joy of problem solving, for as any good math student knows, the chase is better than the catch.

So give Motorhead Math Tutors a try and turn your child into an overnight sensation in math.

University entrance exams are fast approaching, so sign up before it's too late too late!

☆ THE DOOBIE BROTHERS ☆

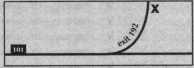

Where every child knows, "We're here to love you."

Hey, moms. What fool believes that good day care is easy to find?
Minute by minute, you're one step closer to quality day care for your little darling.
DON'T DELAY!

Doobie Brothers Day Care

101 ... exit 192 ... X

Start takin' it to the streets, rock on down the highway,
north on the 101, to exit 192, and look for the sign.

FKLA: Elizabeth Kennedy

☆ VAN MORRISON ☆

Van With A Van

Moving. Days like this, you want a man, not a brown eyed girl, to do the job. Someone who will care for things with crazy love, as if they were his own. And that's me! Van Morrison, the Van with a van. Big jobs to small, we will carry on regardless until the job is done. Will work holidays, even Celtic New Year. Don't get stranded with movers that will leave you shaking your head thinking "these are the days". Call Van with a van and I'll come running!* Or rather, driving.

*Except Mystic, CT. My ex-girlfriend Gloria moved there recently, and as a result, I will not take jobs either out of or into the Mystic. Or the surrounding Mystic area. Sorry.

Van w/ Van
203-555-1212

Van w/ van
203-555-1212

Van w/ van
203-555-1212

Van w/ van
203-555-1212

Van w/ Van
203-555-1212

Van w/van
203-555-1212

Van w/ van
203-555-1212

Van w/van
203-555-1212

☆ FLOCK OF SEAGULLS ☆

When '80s New Wave band Flock of Seagulls were just start-ing out in Liverpool, they all shared a flat. This is a letter and photo I discovered from their landlord. Could it really be that the '80s New Wave scene was influenced by some guy named Greg?

HEY, GULLS!

SORRY, HOPE YOU DON'T MIND IF THAT'S WHAT I CALL YOU. SEEMS LIKE A TIME SAVER! ANYHOOZLES, JUST WANTED TO REMIND YOU GUYS THAT RENT IS DUE. NO BIGGIE, I KNOW YOU GUYS ARE STRUGGLING TO MAKE ENDS MEET UNTIL YOU HIT THE BIG TIME (WHICH I KNOW YOU WILL!), BUT IF I COULD GET RENT SOON, THAT WOULD BE GREAT. I'VE HEARD SOME OF THE PRACTICES, SOUNDS GREAT! ALSO, HAVE YOU GUYS DECIDED ON A "LOOK" YET? I KNOW YOU WERE TRYING TO FIGURE IT OUT THE LAST TIME WE TALKED. ANYWAY, IF I COULD GET RENT SOON, THAT WOULD BE SUPER. OH, ALSO, I GOT A NEW HAIR- CUT, WANTED TO SEE WHAT YOU GUYS THOUGHT. I TOOK A PHOTO AND ATTACHED IT SINCE I DON'T GET TO SEE YOU GUYS TOO MUCH. LET ME KNOW WHAT YOU THINK. OKAY, SEE YOU GULLS LATER. JUST KIDDING, I MEAN, SEE YOU GUYS LATER. I SAID "GULLS" BECAUSE THE NAME OF YOUR BAND IS FLOCK OF SEAGULLS.
                                    GREG

☆ SYSTEM OF A DOWN ☆

Sixteen years later, Greg apparently moved to Glendale, California, and ended up being the landlord for the band System of a Down. There are a lot of bands that owe Greg a debt of gratitude. Or should we say, Greg-itude.

HEY, DOWNERS!

SORRY, HOPE YOU DON'T MIND IF THAT'S WHAT I CALL YOU. SEEMS LIKE A TIME SAVER! HEY, THAT REMINDS ME, I USED TO BE THE LANDLORD FOR FLOCK OF SEAGULLS, AND I SHORTENED THEIR NAME ~~TO~~ WHEN I TALKED TO THEM, TOO! ANYHOOZIES, JUST WANTED TO REMIND YOU GUYS THAT RENT IS DUE. NO BIGGIE, YOU GUYS KNOW THAT I LOVE MUSIC AND THAT'S WHY I RENT OUT TO MUSICIANS AND THAT I'M COOL ABOUT IT, BUT IF I COULD GET THE RENT SOON, THAT WOULD BE GREAT. I HEARD YOU GUYS REHEARSING. NOT MY CUP OF TEA, BUT LIVE & LET ROCK, I ALWAYS SAY! HAVE YOU GUYS DECIDED ON A "LOOK" YET? I KNOW IT TAKES MORE THAN THE MUSIC SOMETIMES TO STAND OUT IN THE CROWD, AND IF YOU WANTED MY ADVICE, JUST COME ON BY & KNOCK. OH, ALSO, I DID SOMETHING NEW WITH MY BEARD, WANTED TO SEE WHAT YOU GUYS THOUGHT. I TOOK A PHOTO AND ATTACHED IT SINCE I DON'T GET TO SEE YOU GUYS TOO MUCH. LET ME KNOW WHAT YOU THINK. OH, AND STOP BY AND SAY HI EVERY NOW AND THEN. DON'T BE SUCH DOWNERS. GET IT? BECAUSE YOUR BAND'S NAME IS SYSTEM OF A DOWN.   GREG

☆ FOO FIGHTERS ☆

When Dave Grohl was eleven years old, he supposedly defeated the middle-school bully in an after-school fight. This is a letter from the principal of the school, written to Dave.

JACQUES COUSTEAU
MIDDLE SCHOOL
HOME OF THE BARRACUDAS!

1489 CRACKERTON ROAD
ALEXANDRIA, VIRGINIA 22301

June 14, 1980

TO: David Grohl
FR: Principal Davidson
RE: Apparent after school altercation

David:

It has come to my attention that on June 11, there was an
altercation on school grounds that took place between yourself
and Craig "Foo" Fukowski. In an effort to avoid any punishment
and/or suspension, I'm sure you will deny this. That is fine.

I am just writing to tell you that if it is indeed true that this
fight actually did take place, and if you indeed were the victor
by what has across the board been referred to as a "sound beating",
yo have my sincere and utmost congratulations and respect. As the
victim of several beatings at the hands/fists of the school bully
when I was your age, I was encouraged to hear that someone smaller
(and supposedly weaker) actually stood up for himself and took
matters into his own hands and, better yet, won. Furthermore, as
the principal of a high school, when it comes to matters of the
proper forms of discipline I am allowed to administer to those I
whom I deem worthy, my hands are bound by a heavy dose of moral
and ethical rope. In my opinion, there is no more pure and effective
form of justice than street justice. It's also nice when the
person receiving the justice is a senior, and the person administer-
ing the street justice is a freshman. I guess what I'm trying to
say is, "way to go!"

In any case, I just wanted to drop you a line to express my
gratitude, and thank you personally for helping me maintain order
at Jacques Cousteau High School, even if that wasn't your intention.
This school, and the world in general, could use a few more brave
"Foo" fighters such as yourself.

Of course, if you ever share this letter with anyone, I will deny
that I wrote it, and claim that you broke into my office and stole
some official school stationary and forged this letter.

Have a great summer!

Principal Davidson
Jacques Cousteau Middle School
Go Barracudas!

☆ I LOVE YOU BUT I'VE ☆
☆ CHOSEN DARKNESS ☆

Here is an old letter to lead singer Christian Goyer from an ex-girlfriend, written while they were both in high school. While I can't say for certain, I think this sheds some light on how the band may have come up its their enigmatic name.

My Dearest Christian,

As junior year comes to a close, my heart is filled with both love and sadness. It is filled with love because I have the affections of a wonderful young man. Its filled with sadness because unfortunately, that young man is no longer you. Gary Darkness asked me to prom last week, and I have decided to go with him. I know that you and I have been sort of going out for a few weeks, but Gary's a senior, and...... Oh, Christian, I'm so sorry. I'd be lucky to go to prom with either of you, but I really think Gary could be "the one." Argh, this is so hard!!! I guess the only way to say this is just to say it: Christian, I love you, but I've chosen Darkness. I'm going to prom with Gary. I'm so sorry. I really hope we can still be friends.

Stacy

xoxoxox

☆ PINK FLOYD ☆

Pink Floyd went through what has been described as perhaps the greatest feud in rock and roll history. At the heart of the feud was the band's two main forces, Roger Waters and David Gilmour. It has been stated many times that the band as a whole was not on speaking terms, but most stories seem to indicate Waters was on one side of the feud, and the rest of the band, led by Gilmour, was on the other. There are many theories as to the genesis of the feud, from creative differences to a clash of egos to a philosophical and musical gap. What you are about to read is a transcription of a conversation that took place at perhaps the height of the feud. Waters and Gilmour had gotten to the point where they literally weren't speaking to each other. This was recorded on November 14, 1979, during the recording sessions for their legendary rock opera *The Wall*. Tapes kept rolling in between takes of "Another Brick in the Wall (Part II)." For reference, band members are: Roger Waters (bass), David Gilmour (guitar), Nick Mason (drums), and Richard Wright (keyboards). Rick is the studio's sound engineer.

****** 1 *****

ROGER: All right, that was nice, I think we're close. Rick, can you tell Dave that I want to get another pass at your solo.

RICK: Dave, Roger wants to get another pass at your solo.

DAVE: Right. Tell Roger that we'll do that just as soon as we get back from lunch.

RICK: Roger, Dave would like to do the pass after lunch.

NICK: Yeah, let's grab some chow.

RICHARD: (unintelligible)

DAVE: I could do Mexican.

NICK: What about BBQ?

RICHARD: (unintelligible)

NICK: Ooo, yeah, let's go to KC Rib Ticklers.

DAVE: I'm in. Rick, can you ask Rodge if he's up for barbeque?

RICK: Roger, the guys want to know if you'd like barbeque for lunch.

ROGER: I don't know, I wouldn't mind Indian.

RICK: Roger would like Indian.

DAVE: Oh, come on, that's too heavy, we'll be napping all the rest of the day.

RICK: Uh, Roger, Dave doesn't want Indian. He thinks it's too heavy and might put the band to sleep later.

ROGER: Well, that's what I'm in the mood for. Tell Dave that I'm sorry if he doesn't have what it takes to rise above a good meal and keep rehearsing.

NICK: Oh boy, here we go.

RICHARD: (unintelligible)

DAVE: Uh, you can tell Roger that I have what it takes to rise above a good meal and keep rehearsing, but there's lots of other place to have a good meal besides Indian, which will put us all in a food coma, so what's the point?

Rick: Dave would like to know what the point is.

Roger: Tell Dave that the point is that's what I'm in the mood for, that's what.

Rick: Roger's not in the mood.

Dave: Huh, that's funny. Tell Roger that I thought the point was that 3 of the 4 members of this band wanted KC Rib Ticklers.

Rick: The guys would prefer to go to KC Rib Ticklers.

Roger: Oh, and a heavy barbeque meal isn't heavy?

           (THERE IS A 7 SECOND PAUSE)

****** 2 ******

Roger: (heavy sigh) Ask Dave if he thinks a barbeque meal isn't as heavy?

RICK: You don't think barbeque is as heavy?

DAVE: Not as heavy as Indian.

RICK: Not as heavy as Indian.

ROGER: That's not going to put you in a food coma?

RICK: That's not going to put you in a food coma?

DAVE: Not like Indian, no.

RICK: Not like Indian, no.

ROGER: Look, tell Dave that on "Dark Side of the Moon", he wanted "Speak To Me/Breathe" to be an up tempo number. I told you him it needed to be slow. I knew I wasn't going to convince him with any articulate argument since he's such a stubborn prick, so I made sure we had Indian that day. I think he can agree that we were all pretty tired after, and I think it lent itself well to the final version of the song. The song itself feels sated to me, it's perfect.

            (IT SOUNDS LIKE DAVE AND ROGER ARE ADDRESSING EACH OTHER DIRECTLY AT THIS POINT)

DAVE: Oh, so now you admit that getting Indian was intentional and went against the wishes of the band.

ROGER: Yes, I admit it. But getting Indian was and is for the good of the album, which is bigger than the band. But you're too selfish to realize it, Dave. You just want your KC Rib Ticklers and your Muy Muy Quite Contrary burritos and your Potato and Spud's Fish and Chips*. "Dark Side" wouldn't have turned out as good as it was if not for Indian food.

DAVE: That's bloody fucking rubbish and you know it! That was the first album that we all fully collaborated on which is why it turned out so great and was our first breakthrough album, and you have the fucking nerve to say to our faces that the reason was Indian food? And that Indian food is going to make my solo on "Another Brick" better?

            (THERE IS AN 8 SECOND PAUSE)

DAVE: Roger, is that what you're saying?

RICK: Roger, is that what you're saying?

            (THERE IS A 5 1/2 SECOND PAUS)

ROGER: Yes.

RICK: Yes.

DAVE: Ah, fuck off, we're going to KC Rib Ticklers. Come on, guys.

NICK: I don't know, maybe we should get Indian.

RICHARD: (unintelligible)

☆ BOB SEGER ☆
☆ AND THE ☆
☆ SILVER BULLET BAND ☆

It would appear that Bob Seger's gift for writing great songs came at quite a price. Seger was in psychoanalysis for years to deal with a particular problem that is as shocking as it is enlightening. Here now are his analyst's notes from some of the sessions.

March 17, 1980 - Bob Seger

-subject continues to express feelings of
being a werewolf. Subject is convinced
that when the moon is full, he becomes
a creature of the night

-Subject doesnt particularly care for
long hair and beards, but thinks this
is why his inclination is to wear
his hair long and grow facial hair.
claims it is "instinct", refers to it
as his "day wolf" self.

- subject claims this is the reason
why he named his band "The Silver
Bullet Band". So he never forgets
that he is a werewolf.

- subject claims he woke up naked and
covered in blood, which inspired him
to write the song "Night Moves."

—subject reminds me that werewolves "move in the night... you know, night moves..."

—subject claims he tried to make lyric generic to sound like the story of a human, didn't think people would respond to a song about a werewolf, but the song really is about a werewolf.

—subject reminds me again that werewolves "move in the night ... night moves... night moves"

May 8, 1980 - Bob Seger

—subject claims he woke up
in the Detroit Zoo, in the lion's
den, next to 3 dead lions.

—cites this as ~~~~ inspiration for
the song "Still The Same". Subject
clarifies that while lyrics would
appear to imply the story of a
nemesis or ex-girlfriend who
hasn't changed, the song is actually
about a man who, even though he
wants to believe he is not a werewolf,
is still a werewolf. Or "Still the Same",
as subject says...

—subject claims that touring is booked
in conjunction with the use of
a farmers almanac, to schedule shows
around full moons. subject clarifies

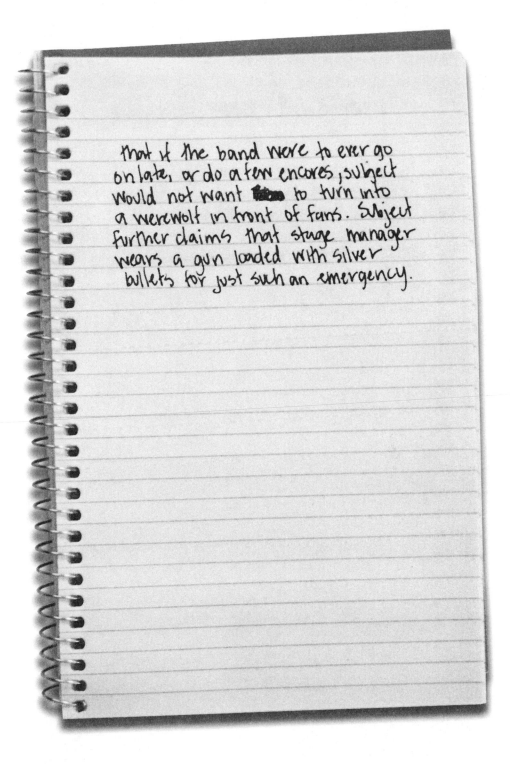

that if the band were to ever go
on late, or do a few encores, subject
would not want ~~them~~ to turn into
a werewolf in front of fans. Subject
further claims that stage manager
wears a gun loaded with silver
bullets for just such an emergency.

August 18, 1980 - Bob Seger

—subject sat silent for the
entire session, until the end,
when he told me that "We've
   got Tonight" is actually a
song about a werewolf.

November 29, 1980

Subject agrees to answer several
"Yes" and "No" questions.

-Are you a werewolf? Yes.

-Have you always been a werewolf? No.

-Is there any chance you are not
   a werewolf? No.

-Do you know the time you became
   a werewolf? No.

-Are all your songs about werewolves? Yes.

-Does the band the Eagles know that
   the song you co-wrote for them,
   "Heartache Tonight," is about a
   werewolf? No.

-Do you ever plan on telling them? No.

—If any of your songs go on to
become the official song of a major
corporation, say for example a
car company, or become massively
famous for being in a movie, would
you tell that corporation or movie
studio that the song they purchased
to promote their product or brand
is actually a song about a werewolf?
                              No.

☆ ROD STEWART ☆

Rod Stewart having his stomach pumped, only to find a mug's worth of semen inside. It is arguably the single greatest urban legend in the world of rock and roll, and it begs only one question: did he or didn't he? The following tour rider* proves once and for all that Rod Stewart *did* in fact ingest a mug's worth of human semen, but not for the reasons that so many have speculated.

---

* I had to drink a mug of cum to obtain this tour rider.

Rod Stewart "Every Tour Tells A Story" Tour Rider
January 14th, 1972
The Orange Bowl, Miami

(this is Rod's rider, please see separate rider for band)

—One box chamomile tea, 5 lemons, and hot water.

—10 boxes cherry Ludens

—5 large towels

—One pot boiling water with eucalyptus leaves

—Please have all chairs and sofas pushed towards the walls.
Rod is an avid footballer and likes to have an open space to
juggle a football before shows to relax.

THE FOLLOWING IS VERY IMPORTANT SO PLEASE MAKE SURE YOU READ THIS
VERY CAREFULLY AND UNDERSTAND THAT YOU MUST NOT SCREW THIS UP:

Mick Waller, the band's drummer, has found that nothing keeps the
kick pedal on his bass drum lubricated like human semen. This is
obviously unconventional, and so it is not discussed publicly. But
many drummers find human semen to be the ideal lubricant for their
kicks. There will be a mug of semen placed backstage on a table for
Mick. Rod likes to keep his mug of tea on the same backstage table,
as he likes to head off stage for quick spot of tea during guitar solos.

******IT IS VERY IMPORTANT THAT YOU KEEP THE MUG OF SEMEN AND THE
MUG OF TEA SEPARATED AND CLEARLY LABELED**********

We have had problems with this in the past. For obvious reasons,
Rod would prefer to not drink the mug of semen. Please take the
necessary steps to make sure that Rod does not drink a mug of semen
when he comes off stage to have some tea. Let me just write this
again so it is very clear. We would like to avoid any situation where
Rod Stewart ends up drinking a mug's worth of semen. Thank you.

☆ THE GUESS WHO ☆

Here is a transcription of an early recording session that seems to shed light on the band's name. The studio engineer must have forgotten to stop the tape (or purposely left it recording?), and it captured a conversation between the band members that took place after a take of "Shakin' All Over." For reference, here are the names of the members of the band at the time this was recorded: Chad Allan (vocals/guitar), Bob Ashley (keyboards), Randy Bachman (guitars), Jim Kale (bass), and Garry Peterson (drums).

CHAD:
Great take, guys, I think we really nailed that one.

ALL:
Yeah . . . here here . . . I agree . . . etc.

BOB:
Yeah, my keyboard is still 'shakin' all over' at how great that take was!

ALL:
(laughter)

RANDY:
Hey, who woulda thought a bunch of guys from Winnipeg would be on their way to making it as rock stars?

ALL:
Yeah . . . I know . . . isn't it great? . . . etc.

JIM:
Yeah, but we still haven't settled on a name.

ALL:
Oh, yeah . . . ah, geeze, that's right . . . yeah, let's get back to that.

GARRY:
Okay, but first, I've got a great knock knock joke.

ALL:
(mumbling disapproval)

CHAD:
Not now, Garry, this is important.

GARRY:
I know, but real quick.

CHAD:
Okay. Real quick.

GARRY:
Okay. Knock knock.

(2)

ALL:
Guess who?

GARRY:
No, you guys always say that when I have a knock knock joke. You
don't say 'guess who', you say 'who's there?"

BOB:
No, it's 'guess who'. See, this is why we never want to do your knock
knock jokes.

GARRY:
Fair enough, but it's 'who's there'.

RANDY:
It's 'guess who'.

GARRY:
It's not. 'Guess who' makes no sense.

CHAD:
Sure it does. Someone knocks at the door, you try to guess who it is.

GARRY:
(exasperated)
You don't try to *guess who it is,* you ask. 'who's there?'. If anything,
the person at the *door* would be the one to say 'guess who'.

JIM:
No.

GARRY:
(sounds figuratively exhausted)
Oh my God. Okay, whatever. You guys can answer the door however
you want. But in the traditional 'knock knock' joke, the response is
"who's there?" Come on, try it. Knock knock.

ALL:
Guess who?

GARRY:
(sounds annoyed)
Knock knock.

ALL:
Guess who?

GARRY:
(sounding more annoyed)
Knock knock.

ALL:
Guess who?

GARRY:
(sounding more annoyed)
Jesus Christ. Knock knock!

ALL:
Guess who?

CHAD:
Wait, I just thought of a name for the band.

☆ THE MODERN LOVERS ☆

Right before he died in 1973, Pablo Picasso wrote a letter to the Modern Lovers, thanking them for their song about him, "Pablo Picasso." This letter has been translated from the Spanish.

To: The Modern Lovers
Fr: Pablo Picasso
Re: "Pablo Picasso"
March 23, 1973

Gentlemen,

I have just listened to a demo of your song "Pablo Picasso". I am not at liberty to
say where I got it, although I understand you are friends with a young man named
John Cale. Nevertheless, I enjoyed it immensely. However, regarding the lyric
"Pablo Picasso was never called an asshole.", which I also thoroughly enjoyed, I
must inform you that this is simply not true. Not only is it not true, but I take
pride in the fact that it is not true! Regardless, I felt compelled, as a new
admirer, to enlighten you as to the inaccuracy. Please indulge a humble old man at
the twilight of his life to correct the error of your ways. Here are all the times
when I was in fact called an asshole.

1906, Paris. Upon completion of my "Portrait of Gertrude Stein", it has been widely
quoted that when somebody commented how Stein didn't look like her portrait, I
famously said "She will." What has not been as widely quoted was that the person
then called me an asshole.

1920, Paris. While working on the ballet Pulcinella with Igor Stravinsky, I told
him that I thought Commedia dell'arte was a boring, lowest common denominator art
form for the masses.
He called me an asshole.

1927, Nice. Upon finding out that I was having a secret affair with a 17 year old
girl named Marie-Therese Walter, my first wife Olga Khokhlova called me an asshole.

1953, Paris. Francoise Gilot, one of my many lovers, whom I met after the liberation
of Paris, left me because of what she called my many indiscretions and unseemly
treatment of her. The last thing she said as she walked out the door was "Picasso,
you are such an asshole."

1955, Paris. After my first wife died, Marie-Therese Walter, the woman I had
started an affair with in 1927, and had a child with in 1935, said she wanted to
get married. I refused, and she called me an asshole.

1961, Vallauris. Francoise Gilot wanted very much to legally legitimize the two children
we had together. I encouraged her to divorce her husband and marry me. She did her
part and filed for divorce, but little did she know that, as my way of getting back
at her for leaving me back in 1953, I had secretly married one of my other lovers,
Jacqueline Roque. When she found out, she called me an asshole.

1967, Chicago. I was commissioned to make a maquette for a 50 foot high public
sculpture. Upon its completion, I was offered payment of $100,000. I refused,
calling it my gift to the city. When I told this to then mayor Richard J. Daley,
he leaned down and whispered in my ear, "What are you trying to be, some kind of
asshole?" He thought I was trying to upstage him, which of course I was not. He
later apologized for calling me an asshole, but this does not take away from the
fact that I was still called an asshole.

And there you have it. The 7 times in my life that I was actually called an asshole.
I don't think it's necessary, but if you want to change the song, that's fine by me. I
just wanted you to know.

Pablo Picasso

☆ THE JESUS ☆
☆ AND MARY CHAIN ☆

During its heyday, the seminal '80s/'90s post-punk band received a letter from a likely/unlikely fan.

SECRETARIAT OF STATE

FROM THE VATICAN, 7 June 1988

Hi, Jim and William.

I have contacted The Vatican and asked The Holy
Father to transcribe and forward this to you.
I am writing to object to the name of your band.

(Before I go any further, let me just say that I
am a huge fan. Love, love, LOVE your guys' sound.
Psychocandy will undoubtedly go down as one of the
most influential, seminal post-punk albums of all
time. Darklands was a brilliant follow up effort,
„Fall" was a standout song for me)

In any case, I just have to be honest and say that
I'm not crazy about the name you've chosen. Don't
get me wrong. I get it. It's ironic, it's edgy,
I'd even say it's clever. But I'd appreciate it if
you'd please reconsider for any albums from here
on. I can't make you change the name, but I'd really
appreciate it. I have instructed His Holiness to
pray for you and future successes for your band.

Okay, okay, take it easy, Jesus, you've said your
piece! 'Preciate your time, and good luck. I'm
excited to hear what else the brothers Reid have in
store for the music loving public!

Anxiously awaiting more but also STRONGLY urging you
to change your name,

Jesus

P.S. - Lose the drum machine. Borrrrr-ing!

☆ THE JAM / ☆
☆ PAUL WELLER ☆

This may very well be the most amazing and unbelievable yet totally real letter in the entire book.

To Mr. Paul Weller:

Good day to you sir. I hope this letter finds
   you well, as I trust it will.

Let me just begin by saying that what you
   are about to read will undoubtedly be
   difficult to comprehend. All I can do is give
   you my word that every word of it is
   the truth.

My name is Thomas Jefferson. As you may or may
not know, I was the third President of the
United States of America. I was was

   also the principal author of the Declaration
of Independence, and indeed, it was I who
pinned the passage. "We hold these truths to be
self-evident, that all men are created equal,
   that they are endowed by their Creator
with certain unalienable Rights, that among these
are Life, Liberty and the pursuit of Happiness."

As remarkable a sentence that has ever been penned
in the history of the written word, it is not
without it's flaws.

Recently, I had a vision. A vision of the future.
Guess who was was was in this vision?

That's right. You. This vision covered your time
in the musical groups The Jam and The Style Council
(really great stuff, by the way). What troubles me most
about this vision is that it occurred after I wrote
the Declaration of Undependance. It troubles me
because the part of the Declaration that says
"all men are created equal" — which I meant when I
wrote it — was completely obliterated and rendered
false when I had this vision. Your unique
blend of talent, charisma, stage presence, sheer
beauty and raw sexuality, especially during the
Style Council Council years, clearly prove to me,

without a shadow of a doubt, that all men are
in fact _Not_ created equal. It has in fact
become, for me, the _only_ truth that I hold to
be self-evident these days, ha ha.
I have wrestled with this vision for some time now.
I have not been able to share this story with anyone.
Surely they would find my claims of a "Jam" and
a "Style Council" and a "Modfather" to be the rantings
of a Lunatic. So I have decided to put my
thoughts to parchment and entrust it with my
family, to be passed on from generation to
generation remaining a family secret until
a Jefferson of your era is able to deliver this
letter to you some 200 odd years later.
I do so hope that this note traveled safely
through history and time and found its
way into your possession. Indeed, I have
instructed any and all of my offspring to
procreate as often as possible to ensure

that the odds of this letter finding its way to you remain high. But I digress.

I wanted you to know that because of your future existence, I could not in good faith let the Declaration of Independence remain as written, lest my legacy be tainted as a man who spoke and tried to intentionally further and promote untruths. That is why I snuck into the home of John Adams, who has been holding onto the Declaration until we find a permanent home for it, and affixed an asterisk next to the passage "all men are created equal". I made it small enough so that no one would notice it unless they were looking for it. But really, there is only one person in the world beside myself who will even know to look for it (wink wink, nudge nudge!).

I wish I had this vision before I wrote the
Declaration, but then again, I wish a lot of things.
I wish some of my slaves weren't so stubborn.
I wish I was born in a time where I was able
    to wear mod style suits like you and
    the guys in The Jam wore. I wish I could
    meet Bruce Foxton. All I can do, is do what
    I can (geeze, it's like great lines just flow
    out of me like water), and that is give my
    best effort to make things right.
It's a small gesture, but hopefully one that
    speaks large volumes to my character.
I felt it my obligation to write to you,
    lest you read the Declaration and think
    me a liar

Best of luck to you. And by the way,
I really love the live version of
"The Combine" on disc 1 of "At The BBC".

Very Sincerely,

Thomas Jefferson

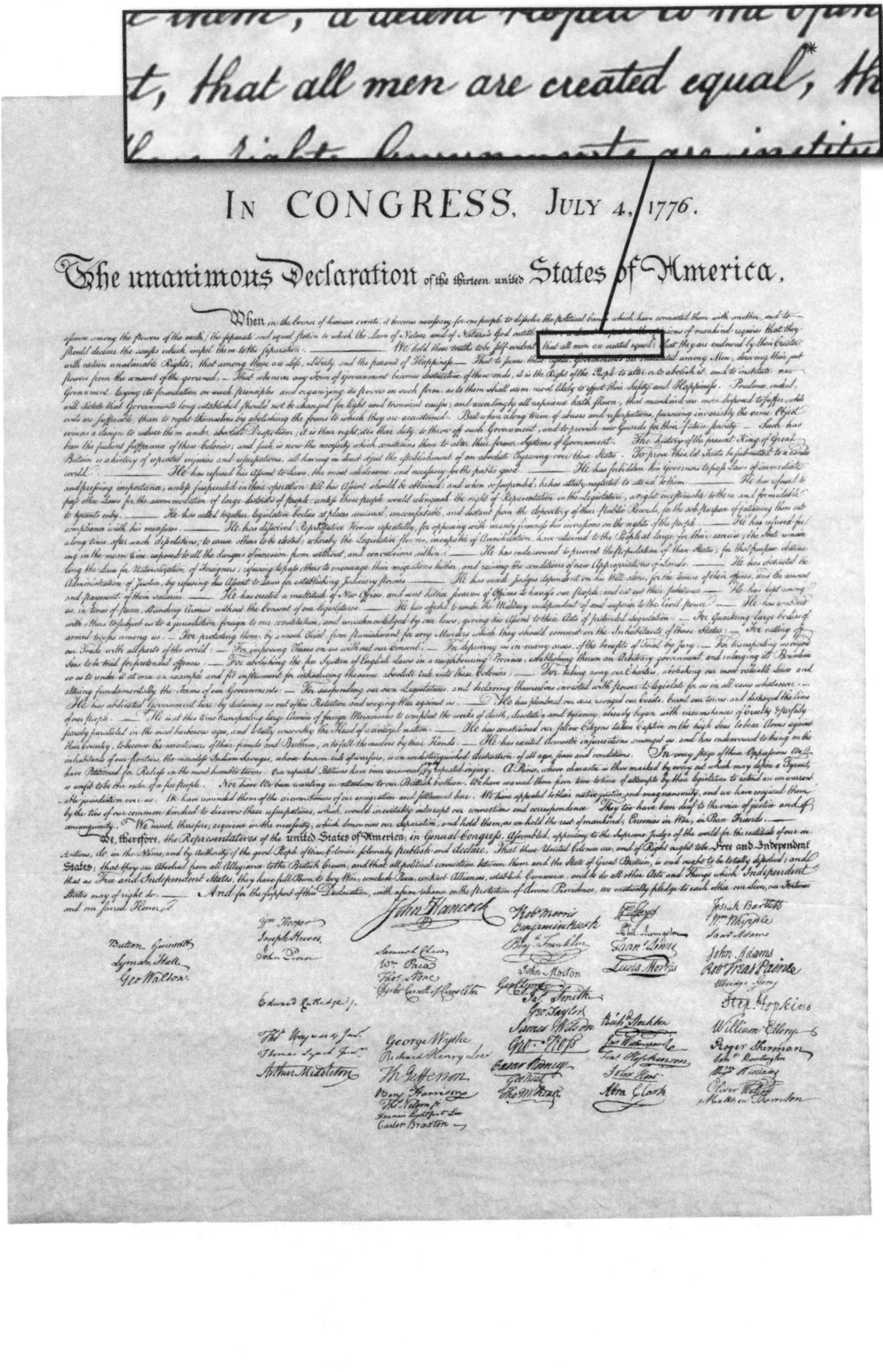
that all men are created equal,*
IN CONGRESS, JULY 4, 1776.
The unanimous Declaration of the thirteen united States of America.

☆ THE WHO ☆

One of the greatest rock bands in music history has one of the great-est, most revered, and most iconic guitar players of its generation. Pete Townsend's unique style included his ubiquitous, influential, and oft-copied "windmill." While it would appear to be purely aesthetic, the by-product of rock and roll attitude and passion, this tour rider reveals that, as is often the case, there is more than meets the eye.

```
                      The Who Tour Rider
                      September 17, 1976
                Charlton Athletic Football Grounds

Please have the following available for the band:

-Backstage fridge must be stocked with water and ice cold Guinness

-Four dozen small terry cloth hand towels for band to use during and
after the show

-Kettle, mugs, lemon, honey and tea for making tea.

-Do not turn on air conditioner before, during, or after show, band
does not like A/C.

-Finger sandwiches must be made available before the show.  Variety of
both meat and cheese sandwiches expected.

-Separate room with cots and white noise machine for pre-show naps.

     THE FOLLOWING IS VERY IMPORTANT AND ALSO CONFIDENTIAL!!!!!!!!
     _PLEASE READ AND SIGN CONFIDENTIALITY WAIVER AT BOTTOM!!!!!!!!

You will not plug in any amps or equipment.  The band does not want,
need or use electricity.  Please find me as soon as the band arrives.
The band has a special generator that they will plug all equipment
into.  After rehearsal, Pete will plug what may or may not be his
penis into said generator (don't ask me how this works, you'll see
at rehearsal).  He will then play guitar and windmill for a half
hour.  The energy he produces via wind power will be stored into the
generator and used to power the show.  The box looks small, but do
not ask questions, as this is highly technical and would take days to
explain.  Just know that it's Pete Townsend, and the power he generates
by windmilling for one show is equivalent to 10 mini-Hiroshimas.  I
know that description is in bad taste, but it is the best way to
describe it.  I know it's the best way to describe it because I've had
this conversation many, many, many times, and have tried to describe it
many different ways.  So please don't ask.  There will also be several
members of the British military on site to oversee the entire ETO
(Energy Transferral Operation), and to also make sure you understand
how confidential this is.  I will tell you now that several event
managers have met with „mysterious deaths" as the result of wanting
to talk about this.  So just be smart, sign this confidentiality
agreement, do your job, and then keep your fucking mouth shut for the
rest of your life.

-We also need a bowl of chocolate truffles next to Keith's drum kit for
the show.

Thanks!  Looking forward to a great show!
```

The Who Tour Rider
September 17, 1976
Charlton Athletic Football Grounds

(p2)

By signing this document on _9-17_ 19_76_ I, agree that I shall never speak
of the events I am about to witness during rehearsal of the band The
Who, specifically, but not withheld to, Pete Townsend as an energy
source. I understand that should I breach this contract, aka open my
dumb fucking mouth, I may meet a suspicious and unsolved murder.

---------------- ---------------------------------
Signature

☆ THE VELVET ☆
☆ UNDERGROUND ☆

The Velvet Underground is one of the most influential bands of all time, and its first album, *The Velvet Underground and Nico*, is one of the most influential albums. Its cover is an instantly recognizable and ubiquitous design, making the group one of the most legendary rock bands ever. Part of the legend is their association with another legend, the artist Andy Warhol, who did the artwork for what has come to be known as "the banana album." What many people don't know is that the album almost came to be known as "the six-foot party sub album," as this was Warhol's original choice for the cover's artwork. Another legend to add to a band already filled with legendary stories is that only Lou Reed approved of the original cover.

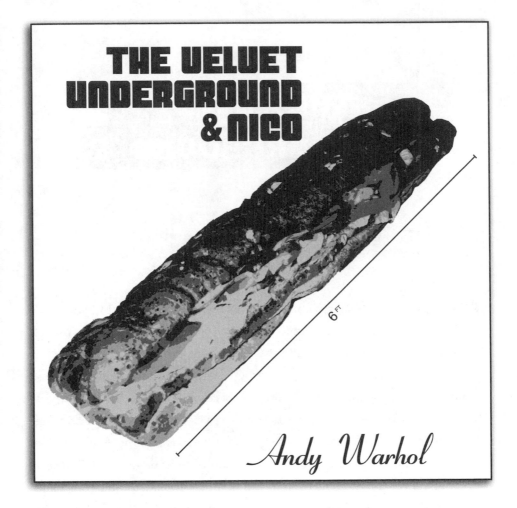

☆ YO LA TENGO ☆

Yo La Tengo has one of the more interesting stories on how it decided on its name, which is based on a Major League Baseball anecdote. When chasing down a fly ball, most baseball players will
yell, "I got it!" Spanish-speaking players of course yell in Spanish, "Yo la
tengo!" In the 1962 season, New York Mets center fielder Richie Ashburn
and Venezuelan shortstop Elio Chacón often collided in the field while
chasing down the same fly ball, due to the language barrier. Ashburn took
to yelling "Yo la tengo!" so his teammate could understand. One game, however, another teammate, left fielder Frank Thomas, who spoke no Spanish,
collided with Ashburn while the two chased down a fly ball. Apparently,
Thomas asked Ashburn after the play, "What's a yellow tango?" The band's
clever, quirky, unique name is as much a trademark as its music. However,
these early rehearsal-session notes show that there were other names in the
running, based on other baseball anecdotes.

BAND NAME IDEAS

"YO LA TENGO"

(based on 1962 Mets season anecdote.
Richie Ashburn and Frank Thomas running
into each other when Ashburn yelled "yo
la tengo!" and Thomas asked him what a
yellow tango was.)

"HAVE YOU SEEN MY MITT?"

(based on 1973 Milwaukee Brewers anecdote.
In a clubhouse prank, left fielder Johnny
Briggs hides catcher Darrell Porter's
catcher's mitt. Porter walks around the
clubhouse all day ~~asking~~ people where his mitt is)
ASKING

"SWEET CLEATS"

(based on 1980 Detroit Tigers anecdote.
The word "sweet" is often used in the
Midwest as slang for something nice, or
cool, or good. Right fielder Kirk Gibson, a
native Midwesterner, upon seeing center
fielder Steve Kemp's new baseball spikes,
apparently said, "Hey, Steve, those are some
sweet cleats." Kemp went on to be known as
"sweet cleats" to his teammates for
the entire season.)

→

Tengo/tango
YO LA TENGO

sweet cleats??

"FUCK YOU, ASSHOLE"

(based on 1983 Baltimore Orioles anecdote,
Observing pitcher Don Welchel's pre-
game ritual of eating a spinach and feta
omelette, outfielder Gary Roenicke
started calling him "Zorba the Greek."
Welchel, not liking the nickname, said
"Fuck you, asshole" to ~~Roe~~ Roenicke.)

maxwell's
653-1703
cbgb 982-4052
dive?
folk city?

☆ THE TONIGHT SHOW ☆

On June 1, 2009, Conan O'Brien took over as host of *The Tonight Show*, replacing long-standing host Jay Leno. Seven months later, NBC announced that due to poor ratings, Jay would be coming back, and Conan was out. It was widely hailed and panned as an absolute debacle that couldn't have been handled worse by NBC. Unrelated to NBC's handling of the situation, but very much part of the transition, longtime *Tonight Show* bandleader Kevin Eubanks announced that he would be resigning. Needless to say, NBC was flooded with inquiries and requests by a number of bands and musicians about becoming the new bandleader or house band for *The Tonight Show*.

TO: JAY LENO
FR: INTERPOL
RE: HOUSE BAND
FEBRUARY 17, 2010.

DEAR JAY.

WE HEAR THAT KEVIN EUBANKS IS QUITTING AS BAND LEADER OF THE TONIGHT SHOW.   WE
WOULD LOVE TO BE YOUR NEW HOUSE BAND. PLEASE LET US KNOW.

THANKS.

PAUL, DANIEL, CARLOS, AND SAM
INTERPOL

 304 HUDSON ST. 7TH FLOOR NEW YORK, NY 10013
212-995-5882 212-995-5883 FAX
www.matadorrecords.com

To: Interpol
Fr: Jay Leno
Re: House Band
February 25, 2010

Interpol:

5! 5! 5! 5! 5! 5! 5! 5! 5!

Hey, guys! Jay Leno here. In case you were confused by all the 5's, I like to start off my letters like I start my show. with a bunch of audience pleasing high-fives! Get it? The 5's are above - or 'higher' - than the text, making them 'high' 5's. Hopefully the 5's never get hurt, although if they do, at least they can get some medical marijuana out here in California and still be 'high' 5's! Heh heh. Hey, that calls for some more 5's.

5! 5! 5! 5! 5! 5! 5! 5! 5!

Anyway, guys, thanks for your letter and interest in becoming the new house band here at The Tonight Show. I checked out some of your music on itunes (and really, shouldn't it be called 'my tunes'? I mean, itunes sounds like something out of a Tarzan movie. I tunes. I Jane!), and I don't think it's the sound we're looking for. We have a pretty rock solid reputation here at The Tonight Show for playing things safe and aiming 100% right down the middle, so I'm not sure my audience is ready for a band whose sound is generally a mix of bass throb and rhythmic, harmonized guitar, with a snare heavy mix. Ha ha. I got that from Wikipedia, I wasn't really sure how to describe you guys. I don't even know what 'bass throb' is, although it certainly sounds like something Tiger Woods probably felt after a night out with one his mistresses! Oh, and speaking of great punchlines, I just can't picture you guys delivering the post-joke chuckles like Kevin.

Although I can't really picture *anybody* doing it as well as he did. Hoo boy, I surely am going to miss The Chuckle Patch.

In any case, thanks again for the interest. I've been getting a lot of inquiries, and I gotta tell ya, if I had a car for every band that wanted to be the new house band on The Tonight Show, I'd have 1/5th the amount of cars I currently have! (Not sure if you know, but I'm known for liking cars, and I own a lot of them)

Anyway, thanks again. If you ever play a show in LA, please let me know so I can be sure to tell some people who might like you're music.

Jay

TO: Jay Leno
FR: Franz Ferdinand
RE: Tonight Show
February 17, 2010

Dear, Mr. Leno.

Congratulations on getting *The Tonight Show* back. While we are sorry
to hear that bandleader Kevin Eubanks will be leaving after a few
months, we would very much like to throw our hats into the ring of
consideration to be the new house band for *The Tonight Show*. It would
be an honour to join the likes of Doc Severson and Kevin Eubanks.

Looking forward to hearing from you.

Franz Ferdinand.

 Domino Recording Company ||||||| *PO Box 47029* ||||||| *London* ||||||| *SW18 1WD*

www.dominorecordco.com

To: Franz Ferdinand
Fr: Jay Leno
Re: House Band
February 26, 2010

Mr. Ferdinand:

Before I get into the letter, I just want to assure you that I promise not to pump (clap),
you up!

Ha ha. Don't know if you remember those Hans and Franz routines from Saturday Night
Live. If you don't remember them or never saw it, the sketch was about two Austrian
bodybuilders named Hans and Franz, and their catch phrase was "We're going to pump
(clap), you up." I put the word 'clap' in parentheses because the two actors playing Hans
and Franz would clap between saying "pump" and "you up". It was very funny, the
characters were modeled after Arnold Schwarzenegger, and were played by Dana Carvey
(Church Lady) and Kevin Nealon (Weeds on Showtime).

In any case, I referenced it because your name is Franz. It's too bad you weren't around
when they were doing Hans and Franz on Saturday Night Live. They could have have
had Kevin Nealon sit out that night, you could have taken his place, put fake muscles
under your clothes, and the sketch could have been called Hans and Franz Ferdinand. Or
Kevin Nealon could have been in it, and it would have been "Hans and Franz and Franz
Ferdinand". Either one would be funny, and either way, you're catch phrase could have
been "We just want to pump (clap), you up, Jacqueline." Ha ha. I have to admit, I don't
really know your music, my assistant gave me a list of your songs, and that one seemed

the funniest to incorporate into the catch phrase. Hey, speaking of which, it's too bad the whole Mark McGuire/Sammy Sosa/Barry Bonds steroids scandal wasn't happening when SNL was doing those characters. Imagine the funny "pump (clap) you up" jokes they could have done about steroids. Hey, speaking of steroids, I'm also pretty curious to see how Mark McGuire does as the St. Louis Cardinals hitting coach this year. Not only will he be able to offer the Cardinal hitters some pretty good advice for getting the bat on the ball, he'll also be able to give them some pretty good advice for getting the needle on the butt!

Okay, on to the point of the letter. I'm sorry to say, but I don't think your music is the right fit for the show. Speaking of which, do you record all the music yourself? There is a lot going on in the songs, and even though it's not my taste, I was impressed that one person could do all of it. If you're ever in LA, I'd love to get lunch and pick (clap), you're brain about that! Not really, I just wanted to make that joke.

To: Rob Thomas
Fr: Jay Leno
Re: New Band Leader
April 16, 2010

Hi, Rob.

Jay Leno here. Don't know if you heard, but I'm doing the Tonight Show again. Also
don't know if you heard, but Kevin Eubanks is stepping down as bandleader. Hey,
speaking of "don't know if you heard", don't know if you heard about this volcano in
Iceland that's causing all these unprecedented flight delays and cancellations. Volcanoes
in Iceland? What's next? Brett Favre permanently retiring from football?

In any case, I'm looking for either a new bandleader, or a new house band. I've been
inundated with requests from bands and musicians that I either have no interest in, or who
are a bad fit for the show. It's getting close to crunch time, and I'm feeling desperate. So
I thought I would reach out to one of my favorite musical acts and see if you had any
interest. I think your musical sensibility would be a perfect fit for the show. The money
is amazing, the schedule is great, I'd let you leave to do any touring you wanted to do,
you could have guest bandleaders...basically, you are my number one choice and I'd give
you carte blanche.

So whadda ya say, buddy? You in? Oh, hey, speaking of "in", I just turned my taxes in
yesterday. Did you know you get a tax break if your car is a hybrid? That's right. I
guess when Heidi Montag heard this, she said "That's great. Can I declare my breasts?"
Anyway, Rob, give it some thought, and let me know asap. Thanks!

rob thomas

To: Jay Leno
Fr: Rob Thomas
Re: Tonight Show
April, 20, 2010

Hi, Jay.

No thanks.

Rob

☆ EPILOGUE ☆

The truth. The truth. If there is one thing I want people to come away with after reading this book, it is simply that. The truth. As stated in the title, this book is filled with 100% irrefutable truth. Just think about that the next time you listen to your favorite band. Yeah, you love their music, but what are they hiding from you? Why are they hiding it? When did they hide it? Where did they hide it? How did they hide it? Who are they hiding it from? The answer to the last question is simple. You. They are hiding it from you. Why? I don't know. I just asked that a few sentences ago. It's one of the questions you need to answer for yourself.

Are Ray and Dave Davies really brothers? Is AC/DC really from Australia? Why is Ted Nugent a Republican? Why did Ric Ocasek write the song "Just What I Needed," when in reality, he felt the exact opposite way? Was Jimi Hendrix's version of "Hey Joe" really about Joe Namath? Did Joe Strummer from the Clash really write down the titles for songs on the back of stamps, paste them to enevelopes, mail the envelopes back to himself, peel off the stamp, and, if he could still read the titles, he would write the songs? These are questions that will hopefully be answered in volume 2 of this book.

But first, that book needs to get pitched. Then it needs to get approved. Then it goes through several drafts, there's lots of editing, legal clearance issues, lunches with my editor, I also have a lot of other things going on, life in general keeps my pretty busy, I've got a kid, and also a dog, and diabetic cat, so it's hard to balance my time between work and family, we wanted to take a vacation this past winter but didn't have time, it was very frustrating, but we're going to aim for a nice trip in the fall, not sure where yet, I'd like to do a snowboarding trip since I haven't gone in awhile, but I'm sure we'll just end up somewhere sunny and warm which will also be just fine, as long as I get to play some golf, even just one round would be great.

My point is, don't rely on me to bring you the truth (actually, *do* rely on me, since that will increase the chances of me getting to write another book). Don't *wait* for me to bring you the truth is what I meant to say. Take a trip to Norman, Oklahoma. Find out where Wayne Coyne lives. Rent a car at the airport. Get insurance for the car if you don't have your own car insurance. Or check with your credit card first, sometimes they provide car insurance on rentals. Once you get the insurance figured out, drive to Wayne's house. Knock on his door. Start asking questions. If you aren't satisfied with the answers he's giving you, ask more questions. Dig. Prod. Don't leave until you get what you came for, even if you didn't know what you were searching for when you arrived. And if Wayne Coyne just happens to be your dad, make sure you find out that he was in the Flaming Lips before he dies.

☆ APPENDIX ☆
Research Photographs

This is me in West Bromwich, England, with Robert Plant's mom. She had the Led Zeppelin napkin. She was a positively lovely woman who made me a delicious dinner of shepherd's pie and biscuits, and a peach cobbler for dessert that was easily the most disgusting thing I've ever eaten. Absolutely fucking horrible.

David Bowie has a house in Zihuatanejo, Mexico. This is me in my hotel gazing out at the Pacific, several hours before meeting with Bowie, wondering if I'm going to head back to the United States empty handed. As you can see, I like to wear my bathing suits '50s style, high above the belly button.

I went to Liverpool, England, to try to find the "Nigel's Linens" that Cream wrote about. It's now a seafood restaurant. Me pointing at this lobster in a tank proves that it's true. There's absolutely no way this photograph could have been taken in Chinatown in New York City, near where I work or anything like that. This photograph was clearly taken in Liverpool, England, at a seafood restaurant that used to be a linen store.

Steven Spielberg promised to give me the Prince set list if I raked the entire lawn at his mansion up in Bar Harbor, Maine. That's his wife, Kate Capshaw, watching me in the foreground, and Steven's texting on his BlackBerry in the background, behind the stop sign. They watched me for the entire seven hours it took. Never said a word. Just watched and made sure I did the entire job, handed me the set list, and went back inside.

Ian Anderson from Jethro Tull played me a flute solo in his living room that was so beautiful and moving I dry-heaved pure emotion for about an hour afterward.

I went to Eugene, Oregon, to meet with Dale Fogerty, John Fogerty's son. I had to beat him four out of seven games of FiFa World Cup '06 before he'd even show me the CCR calendar. I was Brazil. While he was putting his son to bed, I went to custom mode and made a team filled entirely with Pelés, and I absolutely destroyed him four games to none. Ha–ha. Fuck you, Dale. I got the CCR calendar and beat the living shit out of you in FiFa. On Christmas Eve, no less.

This is me and none other than Craig "Foo" Fukowski, outside a Westin Hotel in Potomac, Maryland. Craig told me that he never recovered psychologically from the beating he received at the hands of Dave Grohl, and that he now spends most of his nights masturbating to DVDs of hockey fights and then falling asleep.

Here I am at Martha's Vineyard. I had just met with Eddie Van Halen, and I needed to clear my head when he told me about Bran Fralen. After fifty high speed, ice cold, 'Rona-fueled laps around Nantucket Sound, I was feeling much better.

☆ ACKNOWLEDGMENTS ☆

A big thank you to the following people for their time and help in doing the physical handwriting for some of these totally real documents:

DAVID GLASER – ZZ Top letters
RON COHEN – Bob Dylan
JOHN HODGMAN – David Bowie
JONATHAN JACOBS – Cream
EUGENE MIRMAN – Deep Purple
LEO ALLEN – Jethro Tull
LARRY MURPHY – Kiss
MATT HALL – Led Zeppelin
JOHN LEE – The Rolling Stones
ERIC SLOVIN – MC5
PHIL MORRISON – Grateful Dead
JEFF BUCHANAN – Alice Cooper
MIKE BONFIGLIO – T. Rex
TED SHUMAKER – Santana
JAMES MCNEW – Prince
IRA LAX – Flock of Seagulls/System of a Down
SARAH EGAN – I Love You But I've Chosen Darkness

LESLIE KING – Bob Seger
JIM TOZZI – The Jam
IRA KAPLAN – Yo La Tengo

And a very special thanks to the following people for their part in getting the book made:

John Hodgman. David Rakoff. Christopher Schelling. Allison Lorentzen. Patrick Borelli.

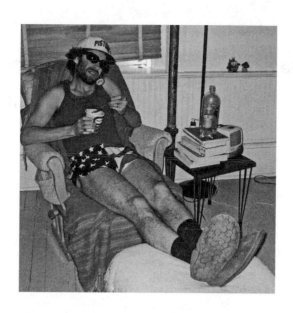

About the Author

Jon Glaser is a writer and actor. He is the creator and star of Adult Swim's *Delocated!*, which he also cowrites and coexecutive produces. As a writer and consultant, Jon's credits include *Late Night with Conan O'Brien*, *The Dana Carvey Show*, *Human Giant*, and *Saturday Night Live*. He has written several stories for the *New York Times Magazine*, and his writing has also appeared in *ESPN The Magazine*, and the book *Howl!* Since this is a book, he isn't going to list his acting credits, which no one gives a shit about anyway.